PARADISE ROW

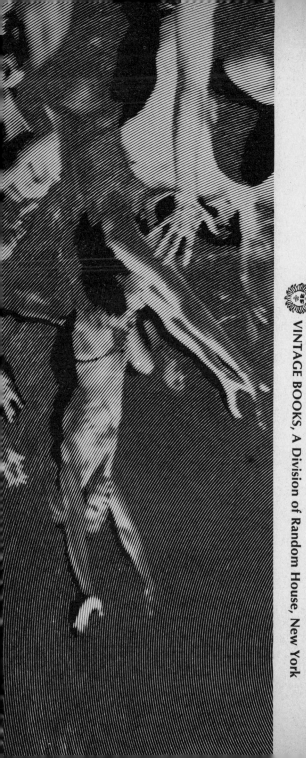

Paradise Now

Collective Creation of The Living Theatre

WRITTEN DOWN BY JUDITH MALINA AND JULIAN BECK

VINTAGE BOOKS, A Division of Random House, New York

VINTAGE BOOKS EDITION, March 1971
Copyright © 1971 by Judith Malina and Julian Beck

ISBN: 0–394–71101–7
Library of Congress Catalog Card Number: 74–140718

Manufactured in the United States of America

The play "Paradise Now" is not private property:
there are no performance royalties to pay:
it is free:
for any community that wants to play it.

Acknowledgment is gratefully extended to the following for
permission to reprint from their works:

Princeton University Press: THE I CHING, OR BOOK OF
CHANGES, translated by Richard Wilhelm, rendered into
English by Cary F. Baynes, Bollingen Series XIX. Copyright
1950, © 1967 by Princeton University Press.
Schocken Books, Inc.: TEN RUNGS: HASIDIC SAYINGS, by
Martin Buber. Copyright 1947 by Schocken Books, Inc.
Penguin Books Ltd.: THE POLITICS OF EXPERIENCE, by R. D.
Laing. THE NATURE OF THE UNIVERSE, by Lucretius,
translated by R. E. Latham.

The collective creation of "Paradise Now" is the work of

Jim Anderson	Steven Ben Israel
Pamela Badyk	Birgit Knabe
Cal Barber	Mary Krapf
Julian Beck	Sandy Linden
Rod Beere	Judith Malina
Carol Berger	Michele Mareck
Odile Bingisser	Gianfranco Mantegna
Mel Clay	Günter Pannewitz
Rufus Collins	Dorothy Shari
Pierre Dévis	William Shari
Echnaton	Luke Theodore
Carl Einhorn	Steve Thompson
Gene Gordon	Jim Tiroff
Roy Harris	Diana Van Tosh
Jenny Hecht	Petra Vogt
Frank Hoogeboom	Karen Weiss
Henry Howard	Peter Weiss
Nona Howard	Souzka Zeller

Writing down "Paradise Now" did not begin until six months after the premiere. This means that it was not read by the actors until more than a year later, when the writing was completed, more than fifty performances after the premiere.

The Living Theatre thanks Gianfranco Mantegna for seeing this manuscript through to publication.

The world premiere of "Paradise Now" took place in Avignon in the Cloître des Carmes, under the auspices of the Festival d'Avignon, on July 24, 1968.

PARADISE NOW

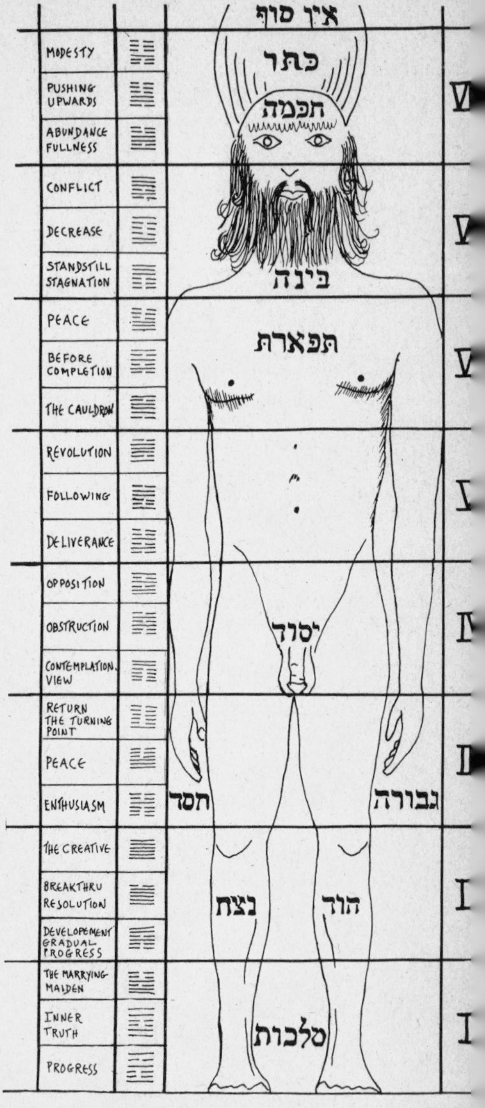

MODESTY	
PUSHING UPWARDS	
ABUNDANCE FULLNESS	
CONFLICT	
DECREASE	
STANDSTILL STAGNATION	
PEACE	
BEFORE COMPLETION	
THE CAULDRON	
REVOLUTION	
FOLLOWING	
DELIVERANCE	
OPPOSITION	
OBSTRUCTION	
CONTEMPLATION. VIEW	
RETURN THE TURNING POINT	
PEACE	
ENTHUSIASM	
THE CREATIVE	
BREAKTHRU RESOLUTION	
DEVELOPEMENT GRADUAL PROGRESS	
THE MARRYING MAIDEN	
INNER TRUTH	
PROGRESS	

אין סוף

כתר

חכמה

בינה

תפארת

יסוד

חסד · גבורה

נצח · הוד

מלכות

THIS CHART IS THE MAP

THE LIVING THEATRE

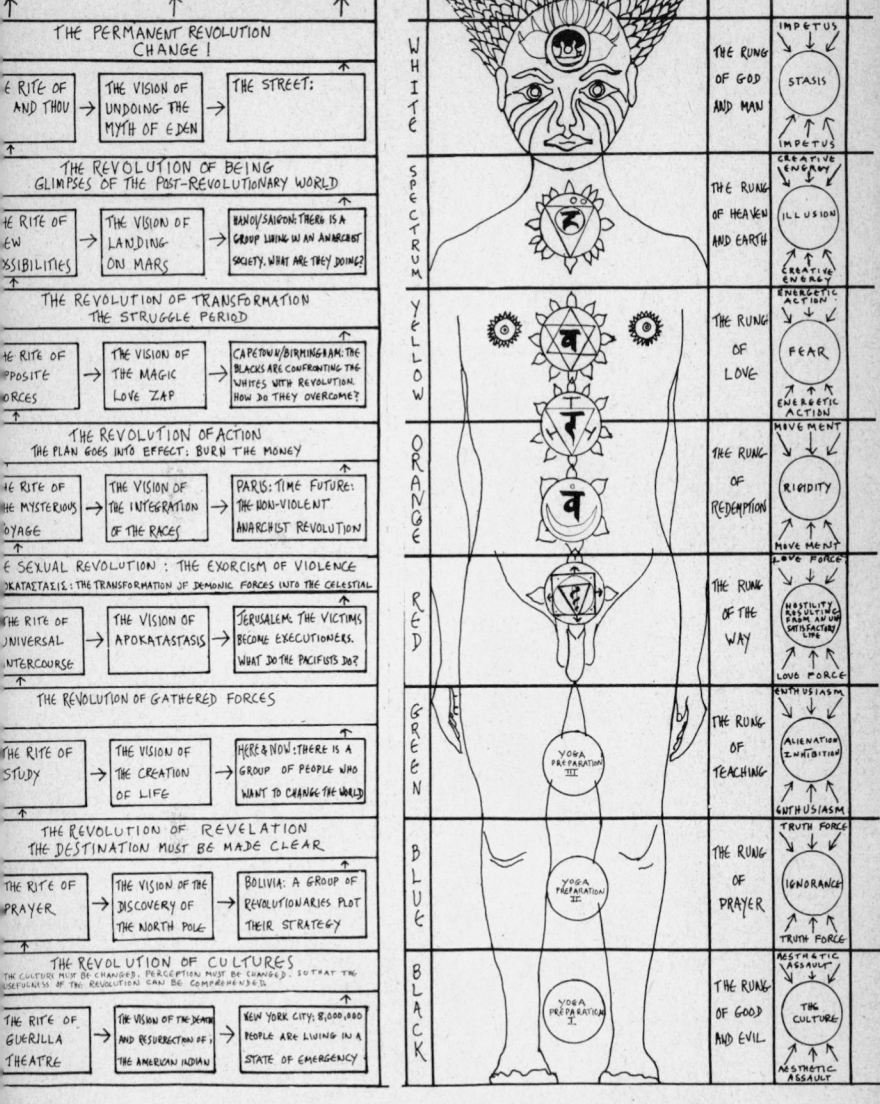

THE PERMANENT REVOLUTION
CHANGE!

E RITE OF | THE VISION OF | THE STREET:
AND THOU | UNDOING THE
| MYTH OF EDEN

THE REVOLUTION OF BEING
GLIMPSES OF THE POST-REVOLUTIONARY WORLD

E RITE OF | THE VISION OF | HANOI/SAIGON: THERE IS A
EW | LANDING | GROUP LIVING IN AN ANARCHIST
SSIBILITIES | ON MARS | SOCIETY. WHAT ARE THEY DOING?

THE REVOLUTION OF TRANSFORMATION
THE STRUGGLE PERIOD

E RITE OF | THE VISION OF | CAPETOWN/BIRMINGHAM: THE
PPOSITE | THE MAGIC | BLACKS ARE CONFRONTING THE
ORCES | LOVE ZAP | WHITES WITH REVOLUTION.
| | HOW DO THEY OVERCOME?

THE REVOLUTION OF ACTION
THE PLAN GOES INTO EFFECT: BURN THE MONEY

E RITE OF | THE VISION OF | PARIS: TIME FUTURE:
HE MYSTERIOUS | THE INTEGRATION | THE NON-VIOLENT
OYAGE | OF THE RACES | ANARCHIST REVOLUTION

E SEXUAL REVOLUTION: THE EXORCISM OF VIOLENCE
OKATASTASIS: THE TRANSFORMATION OF DEMONIC FORCES INTO THE CELESTIAL

THE RITE OF | THE VISION OF | JERUSALEM: THE VICTIMS
UNIVERSAL | APOKATASTASIS | BECOME EXECUTIONERS.
NTERCOURSE | | WHAT DO THE PACIFISTS DO?

THE REVOLUTION OF GATHERED FORCES

THE RITE OF | THE VISION OF | HERE & NOW: THERE IS A
STUDY | THE CREATION | GROUP OF PEOPLE WHO
| OF LIFE | WANT TO CHANGE THE WORLD

THE REVOLUTION OF REVELATION
THE DESTINATION MUST BE MADE CLEAR

THE RITE OF | THE VISION OF THE | BOLIVIA: A GROUP OF
PRAYER | DISCOVERY OF | REVOLUTIONARIES PLOT
| THE NORTH POLE | THEIR STRATEGY

THE REVOLUTION OF CULTURES
THE CULTURE MUST BE CHANGED. PERCEPTION MUST BE CHANGED. SO THAT THE
USEFULNESS OF THE REVOLUTION CAN BE COMPREHENDED.

THE RITE OF | THE VISION OF THE DEATH | NEW YORK CITY: 8,000,000
GUERILLA | AND RESURRECTION OF: | PEOPLE ARE LIVING IN A
THEATRE | THE AMERICAN INDIAN | STATE OF EMERGENCY

| | | SPECTRUM | | | |

WHITE — THE RUNG OF GOD AND MAN — IMPETUS / STASIS / IMPETUS
SPECTRUM YELLOW — THE RUNG OF HEAVEN AND EARTH — CREATIVE ENERGY / ILLUSION / CREATIVE ENERGY
YELLOW — THE RUNG OF LOVE — ENERGETIC ACTION / FEAR / ENERGETIC ACTION
ORANGE — THE RUNG OF REDEMPTION — MOVEMENT / RIGIDITY / MOVEMENT
RED — THE RUNG OF THE WAY — LOVE FORCE / HOSTILITY RESULTING FROM AN UNSATISFACTORY LIFE / LOVE FORCE
GREEN — THE RUNG OF TEACHING — ENTHUSIASM / ALIENATION INHIBITION / ENTHUSIASM
BLUE — THE RUNG OF PRAYER — TRUTH FORCE / IGNORANCE / TRUTH FORCE
BLACK — THE RUNG OF GOOD AND EVIL — AESTHETIC ASSAULT / THE CULTURE / AESTHETIC ASSAULT

YOGA PREPARATION III

YOGA PREPARATION II

YOGA PREPARATION I

SENTIAL TRIP IS THE VOYAGE FROM THE MANY TO THE ONE   THE PLOT IS THE REVOLUTION

PARADISE NOW   COLLECTIVE CREATION

The play is a voyage from the many to the one and from the one to the many. It is a spiritual voyage and a political voyage. It is an interior voyage and an exterior voyage. It is a voyage for the actors and the spectators. It begins in the present and moves into the future and returns to the present. The plot is The Revolution.

The voyage is a vertical ascent toward Permanent Revolution.

The Revolution of which the play speaks is The Beautiful Non-Violent Anarchist Revolution.

The voyage is charted. The Chart is the map. The Chart depicts a ladder of eight Rungs. Each Rung consists of a Rite, a Vision, and an Action which lead to the fulfillment of an aspect of The Revolution. The Rites are physical/spiritual rituals/ceremonies which culminate with a Flashout. The Visions are cerebral. They are images, symbols, dreams. The awareness which issues from the experience of the Rite and the awareness which issues from the experience of the Vision merge to precipitate the Action. The Actions are enactments of political conditions performed by the spectators and the actors. These conditions are specified as taking place in a particular city but lead to revolutionary action here and now. The Rites and Visions are performed by the actors, but the Actions are introduced by the actors and are performed by the public with the help of the actors. The Actions are introduced by a text spoken by the actors.

The purpose of the play is to lead to a state of being in which non-violent revolutionary action is possible.

The Chart contains information drawn from the Kabbalah, Tantric and Hasidic teaching, the I Ching, and other sources. The information on the Chart is arranged to aid the vertical ascent and to serve as a guide during the voyage. The Chart is designed so that it can be extended horizontally with any additional information that seems useful.

THE SOCIAL AND POLITICAL REVOLUTIONS

Each Rung is an element of a dialectic of Revolution. The first four are steps which culminate in The Revolution of Action, marking the beginning of Anarchist social-restructure and the end of Capitalism and The State. At all points in the performance the actor's superobjective is to further radical action demonstrating the futility of violence and the joyous quality of non-violent revolutionary action. At all points the superobjective is to work for the changes that diminish violence both in the individual and in the exterior forms of society. The Revolution in all its stages is counterviolent and seeks the emergence of a state of being in which the causes of violence are no longer active and therefore in which the expression of violence is no longer necessary. The first four Rungs occur (both politically and in the play) in sequence and simultaneously. The Revolution of Cultures (Rung I), which consists fundamentally of changing and assaulting the Culture so that the people can begin to be open to change, continues to take place while the purposes of The Revolution are being explained (The Revolution of Revelation, Rung II).

The actors take as a premise that no revolutionary action can be fulfilled externally (socially/economically/politically) without a parallel change within the revolutionary himself. Nor can any true interior fulfillment be found for the individual if he disregards the social/economic/political conditions of the world in which he lives. The Revolution must therefore be both an Interior and an Exterior Voyage, a Personal and a Supra-Personal Voyage, a Spiritual and a Political Voyage, a Psychological and an Economic Voyage, a Philosophical and a Social Voyage, an Individual and a Collective Voyage.

The Revolution seeks to establish a State of Being of Interdependence between the Individual and the Collective, in which the Individual is not sacrificed to the Collective nor the Collective to the Individual. It is the premise of The Revolution that exterior changes or interior changes independent of each other are not sufficient. Exterior political change, for instance, without concomitant individual spiritual change cannot resist corruption. Nor can individual interior spiritual change be uncorrupt if the world on which the individual depends for subsistence remains unchanged.

Preparation for the revolutionary voyage implies that the actor make a study of both revolutionary and spiritual thought and teaching.

THE PHYSICAL BODY

Discovery and use of the body so that feelingful physical awareness can be unified with thought is an essential revolutionary voyage. As the actor proceeds from Rung to Rung he seeks to experience that region of the body corresponding to that Rung and to free it of its taboos. At the end of the journey the actors' and spectators' bodies should be ready for action.

THE I CHING

The I Ching was consulted twenty-four times, once for each Rite, Vision, and Action. The oracles were arrived at by Steve Thompson by following the method of the coin oracle. The actual text consulted was Richard Wilhelm's German transla- tion of the Chinese, rendered into English by Cary F. Baynes.

The oracles, arrived at by chance, give the actors who study them the wisdom of the ancient Chinese sages to guide them step by step as they encounter by chance the unplanned events that certainly occur during the course of the voyage.

THE HASIDIC RUNGS

It was the Hasidim who conceived of life as if it were lived on the rungs of a ladder that connects earth to heaven. The rungs refer to different kinds of action and states of being. The order in which the rungs are vertically arranged is not prescribed, but the assumption is that if one were to traverse all of them one would unify heaven and earth. The Hasidim also believe that the same thing is possible from any point on the ladder: that suddenly God can catch hold of you and pull you up to the top.

Martin Buber's studies of this aspect of Hasidic thought led him to collect the sayings of the Hasidim which were "scat- tered through hundreds of books in versions largely distorted in the speech and writings of the disciples who transmitted them." Those related specifically to the concept of the rungs he collected in a volume called "Ten Rungs: Hasidic Say- ings"; and this is the source of the citations used to serve among the Guides for the Rungs of "Paradise Now." The English translation was made by Olga Marx.

Of the Concept of the Ladder and its Rungs,
the Hasidim say:

"There is no rung of being on which we cannot find the holiness of God everywhere and at all times."

"Man is a ladder placed on the earth and the top of it touches heaven."

"The souls descended from the realm of heaven to earth, on a long ladder. Then it was taken away. Now, up there, they are calling home the souls. Some do not budge from the spot, for how can one get to heaven without a ladder? Others leap and fall and leap again, and give up. But there are those who know very well that they cannot achieve it, but try over and over again until God catches hold of them and pulls them up."

"No limits are set to the ascent of man, and to each and everyone the highest stands open. Here it is only your personal choice that decides."

THE COLORS

The colors move from darkness to brightness. Each Rung is suffused with its own special illumination. The colors are illuminations designed to unify the consciousness and associations of everyone present. The Rites are performed in varying degrees of white light and darkness. Each Vision is lit in the color of the Rung, and each Action is lit by the color of the Rung with some white light added to increase the sense of the here and now. White light is always turned on in the audience area when the Actions begin.

THE CHAKRAS

The Vedas, the Upanishads, the Tantra Shastras, and other sacred Hindu texts describe six major concentrations or centers (Chakras: literally, wheels) of physical and metaphysical power located inside the physical body of every human being, power which encompasses all of human thought, feeling, and expression. The Chakras, they say, contain essences of all the things and appearances of the universe. All of these are only partially comprehended or experienced during the normal course of existence. The purpose of the practice of Yoga (Union) is to raise these powers to a state of Pure Consciousness and Unification which, say the sacred texts, lead the practitioner into a state of Supreme Bliss. It is a process of exchanging worldly experience for unlimited comprehension.

In order to arrive at this state it is necessary to arouse the dormant powers in the body and to comprehend them through will, knowledge, and action, to surpass them, going on to higher and more profound experience until all experience has been aroused to consciousness which leads to a state of being in which the Yogi experiences oneness-in-and-with-everything, Total Consciousness, Supreme Peace.

The Chakras are located in specified physical locations in the body starting at the base of the spine and culminating in the upper cerebrum of the brain. As the practitioner passes from one Chakra to the next all that he has aroused and experienced dissolves in a state of balance in which object and subject disappear and only the One remains.

The basic activating power is called Kundalini. She is the power with which each individual activates experience. Because ordinarily each individual does not experience life fully, her condition is described as dormant, and she rests like a sleeping snake coiled up in the lowest of the six Chakras.

The first three Rungs are Yoga Preparations because the first Chakra is located in the perineum (between the anus and the sexual organs) and is the primary energy source. In order to awaken this energy source (Kundalini), the practice of Hatha Yoga, Raja Yoga, and Mantra Yoga are prerequisite.

It is thru the practice of Yoga that Kundalini is aroused and begins her ascendant voyage until she reaches the sixth Chakra and unites with Shiva, the Self as Pure Consciousness. Beyond this there is yet another Chakra, the seventh, which when entered unites the individual with the Limitless.

After entering the sixth Chakra, Kundalini usually descends to the first Chakra, reactivating the awareness which dissolved as she rose, leaving the Yogi with a developed mundane consciousness with which to confront gross life.

THE CONFRONTATIONS

The Confrontations are an attempt to define and thereby understand the characteristics of the stumbling block at each Rung, and of the form of action that can overcome it. Thus at the beginning the stumbling block is The Culture which is overcome by Aesthetic Assault; and at the end the stumbling block is Stasis which is overcome by Impetus. The Confrontations are guides to the relationship between the actor and the public at each stage of the trip. The Resistance to the Revolutionary Change is treated as the obstacle. The energy form designated is an appropriate strategy for the actor to use to transform the obstacle.

THE KABBALAH

The classical Kabbalists devised 10 designations for the Attributes of The Holy One which they called the 10 Sefiroth (Emanations). To demonstrate the 10 Holy Attributes they projected a figure called Adam Kadmon, the Celestial Adam, in whose image The Holy One made Man, the Earthly Adam.

The Kabbalists then showed the correspondence of the 10 Holy Attributes to the form of this structure thus:

1	Kether	The Crown	The Highest Achievement
2	Chokmah	The Brow	Wisdom
3	Binah	The Throat	Understanding
4	Chesed	The Right Arm	Mercy
5	Geburah	The Left Arm	Severity
6	Tifereth	The Stomach	The Essence (Beauty)
7	Netzach	The Right Leg	Triumph
8	Hod	The Left Leg	Glory
9	Yesod	The Sex	The Foundation
10	Malkuth	The Feet	The Kingdom

Above all these is En Sof, The Endless.

In the structure for "Paradise Now" the 10 Holy Attributes (The Sefiroth) are arranged in eight Rungs as follows:

1	Malkuth	as The Feet is	The Kingdom	Rung I
2	Hod & Netzach	as The Legs are	Glory & Triumph	Rung II
3	Chesed & Geburah	as the Hands (The Arms) are	Mercy & Severity	Rung III
4	Yesod	as The Sex is	The Foundation	Rung IV
5	Tifereth	as The Stomach is	The Essence	Rung V

6 Tifereth	as The Heart is	Beauty	Rung VI
7 Binah	as The Throat is	Understanding	Rung VII
8 Chokmah	as The Brow	Wisdom & The	
& Kether	as The Crown are	Highest Achievement	Rung VIII

En Sof, The Endless = The Permanent Revolution

At each Rung the actors use their knowledge of these Sefiroth to enact the scene. They can use the imagery of the structure of Adam Kadmon focusing on the Holy Attributes applicable to the Rung they have reached, and at the same time refer to the physical entity of their own bodies as being the image of the Holy Structure. This focuses the energies of their performance on a specific part of the body, ascending as the performance progresses from below to above (Feet to Head to Infinity), and concentrating the attention to the Attributes of Holiness, which are God's and can become Man's.

RUNG I
The Rung of Good and Evil

How
The Rite of Guerilla Theatre
and
The Vision of the Death and Resurrection of the American
    Indian
lead to
Action I: New York City: (8,000,000 people are living
                          in a state of emergency and
                          don't know it.)

and
THE REVOLUTION OF CULTURES:
The Culture must be changed. Perception must be
changed. So that the usefulness of The Revolution can be
understood.

Physical Focus: The Feet

I Ching Oracles: For the Rite: Progress
                For the Vision: Inner Truth
                For the Action: The Marrying Maiden

Color: Black

Yoga Preparation I: Asana Yoga (Physical Postures)

Confrontation: The Culture × Aesthetic Assault

Kabbalistic Sefirah: Malkuth (The Kingdom)

Rite I
THE RITE OF GUERILLA THEATRE

When the audience has almost completely assembled, the actors enter the theatre, mingling with the spectators in the aisles and on the stage and in the lobby. Each actor approaches a spectator and, addressing him individually, speaks the first of five phrases directly to him. At first he speaks in a very quiet, urgent, but personal voice.

PHRASE 1

I AM NOT ALLOWED TO TRAVEL WITHOUT A PASSPORT.

He goes from spectator to spectator and repeats this phrase. With each repetition, his voice and body express greater urgency and frustration. He speaks only this phrase. If the spectator addresses him, he listens to the spectator but repeats only this phrase. The spectator may mock him, encourage him, question him. The spectator may be passive, sympathetic, superficial, witty, profound, cynical, hostile. The actor uses this response to increase his expression of the frustration at the taboos and inhibitions imposed on him by the structure of the world around him. He is obsessed with the meaning of the prohibition and by the ramifications of the prohibition. He cannot travel freely, he cannot move about at will, he is separated from his fellow man, his boundaries are official: the Gates of Paradise are closed to him.

He hears his fellow actors flipping out and is affected by the community of protest. He experiences the spectators' growing frustration at the sense of a lack of communication. By the end of two minutes, all of the actors have reached a point close to hysteria. They are shouting the words with anguish and frustration. They are flipping out. The Cherub with the Flaming Sword is standing at the frontiers and at the customs stations. At the end of two minutes the actors go beyond words into a collective scream. This scream is the pre-revolutionary outcry. (Flashout.)*

At this point the actors return to the artist's quiet center. They stand still and breathe.

Pause and begin again.

PHRASE 2

I DON'T KNOW HOW TO STOP THE WARS.

Again each actor begins by addressing the spectators quietly and personally. He expresses his own passionate frustration at his inability to abolish even the most obvious evil: War. His guilt, his responsibility, his need. He cries out against the system and the culture which block his peacemaking efforts. The spectators' response, whether negative, positive, or passive, increases his horror at his inability to stop the killing. Passion and frustration mount in crescendo until they reach the point of the collective scream. (The Flipout and Flashout.)

Pause and begin again.

PHRASE 3

YOU CAN'T LIVE IF YOU DON'T HAVE MONEY.

Beginning quietly and personally the actors repeat this phrase. Two minute crescendo. There is no way to sustain

---

* Whenever this happens in the play, the actor by the force of his art approaches a transcendent moment in which he is released from all the hangups of the present situation.

yourself on this planet without involvement in the monetary system. The actors see in the spectators' responses the floundering economics of the structure. It makes them crazy. It makes them crazy to realize that many spectators do not know that they are talking about death by starvation. Et cetera. (Flipout. Scream. Flashout.)

Pause and begin again.

PHRASE 4

I'M NOT ALLOWED TO SMOKE MARIJUANA.

Two minute crescendo. From the horror of death by starva- tion to the horror at the prohibition of pleasures. (The same legislators sign the bills that permit napalm and prohibit pornography.) The sense of living in an insane world mounts. The Culture of Laws and Prohibitions is making us crazy. (Flipout. Scream. Flashout.)

Pause and begin again.

PHRASE 5

I'M NOT ALLOWED TO TAKE MY CLOTHES OFF.

Two minute crescendo. Even the nearest, the most natural, is prohibited. The body itself of which we are made is taboo. We are ashamed of what is most beautiful; we are afraid of what is most beautiful. The corruption of the fig leaf is com- plete corruption. We may not arouse each other; we may not act naturally toward one another. The Culture represses Love. (Flipout.)

Having come to the final human absurdity that the body is somehow bad, the actors do not scream about it, but act it out by removing as much of their clothing as the law allows. As they reach the climax of their flipout they begin to tear their clothes off in a frenzy while shouting out I'M NOT AL-

LOWED TO TAKE MY CLOTHES OFF. They are left standing in the aisles and on the stage, the forbidden areas of their bodies covered, the rest exposed. It is an active demonstration of the Prohibition. When the action has reached this legal limit, the actors say once more I'M NOT ALLOWED TO TAKE MY CLOTHES OFF and flash out. They are standing outside the Gates of Paradise. First Assault on the Culture. (Flash-out.)

THE SIGNAL

At the end of this Rite, as at several other points in the course of the voyage, any actor who feels like it, who is so moved, can make a signal to everyone present.

The signal can be a sound, a word, a gesture, a look, all or any of these. The signal is intended to locate and communicate where the actor is at in relation to himself, his surroundings, the performance, and everyone else. It is usually brief. One or more actors may signal at the designated points, or in fact at any point at which the actor feels that a signal is called for and that he is capable of it.

Vision I
THE VISION OF THE DEATH AND RESURRECTION OF THE AMERICAN INDIAN

LIGHT: The lights in the theatre go down. It is dark. In the playing area there is a dim light.

IMAGE: The light of the open fire in the middle of the dark forest.

The actors gather on stage. They sit cross-legged, silent, in a ceremonial circle. They pass pipes from one actor to the

other. They smoke the pipe of peace until they become Indians. They flashout.

One by one the actors rise and take positions for the formation of totem poles. At a cue from one actor (Shaman) they
suddenly form five totem poles facing the public. The totem

poles consist of four actors each. The bottom man crouches low; the second man stands above and behind the first, his legs spread wide; the third man stands close behind the second and carries a fourth man on his shoulders. They are the figures on the totem poles, grimacing, supernatural, animistic, fetishistic, demonic, celestial. They remain motion-

less for a short time. Then the totems begin to move; slowly
they advance, beating a rhythm with their feet. They are the
Emergence of Natural Man, and as they move forward one by
one, the murderous shots of civilization ring out and they are
shot down, each one making the sound of the bullet and the
sound of the Indian's scream as he falls forward face down
onto the stage, biting the dust.

IMAGE: The Fallen, the Slain Red Man.

Pause.

Action I

The Action and its Text: the Text describes the basic conditions. Its purpose is stimulus, suggestion, challenge, en-
couragement, to enable the public to enact the revolutionary
situation of each Rung. The Text is a call to action.

Each Text is related to a specific geographical location in
which the revolutionary situation which relates to that Rung
is projected. The lines of the Text make use of specific references, quotations, and dialectic tenets and questions relating to that stage. The Text also refers to the relevant body
parts of the Tantric Figure and of Adam Kadmon. It makes
suggestions for theatrical enactment by the spectator/par-
ticipants, as well as suggesting subject matter for speech and
dialogue.

The Text is spoken by and divided among the actors of the
company. At the end of The Vision of the Death and Resurrection of the American Indian, the actors are lying face down
on the playing area. The actors remain lying prone and as
each actor speaks he lifts his head and shoulders, supporting
his weight with his arms, and delivers his lines loudly and
clearly to the public, and sinks back again to his prone position.

New York City.

How The Rite of Guerilla Theatre and The Vision of the Death and Resurrection of the American Indian lead to The Revolution of Cultures.

Free theatre. The theatre is yours. Act. Speak. Do whatever you want.

Free theatre. Feel free. You, the public, can choose your role and act it out.

New York City. Eight million people are living in a state of emergency and don't know it.

Manhattan island is shaped like a foot.

At the foot of New York is Wall Street.

Free theatre. In which the actors and the public can do anything they like.

Free theatre. Do whatever you want with the capitalist culture of New York.

Free theatre. How much did you pay to get in here?

Act.

Enter: the spirit of two million blacks.

When you criticize radically, you construct.*

Act. Find the pain. Feel it. Make the sound of it.

Don't step on the Indians.

Be the culture.

What is The Revolution of Cultures?

How does it feel on your back, in your head, underfoot?

* From an interview with Daniel Cohn-Bendit printed in "Le Nouvel Observateur." The interview was conducted by Pierre Hahn.

Be the police.

Be a foot.

Express the point of view of the Maoists.

What is to be done?

Show the violence. Show the anti-violence. Be the Statue of Liberty.

Don't step on the Indians.

Be the forces of repression.

Be the students at Columbia.*

Undo the Culture.

Listen. Under the pavement of New York you can hear the Indians.

Enact the culture of New York. Change it.

* The reference is to the student revolt at Columbia University in April 1968.

The actors are still lying prone. They now wait one minute for the public to do anything it wishes to do. The public reacts. Anytime after one minute that there is a lull in the sound and activities of the public, the actors begin to beat a rhythm with their knees on the stage floor as they lie prone (and otherwise motionless). It is the rhythm of an Indian dance.

IMAGE: The earth, the pavement, is throbbing.

PHASE II

Note: Phase II is an additional text to be used when the reaction of the public calls for it.

Form counter-societies.

Create a parallel culture, and, underneath, a sub-culture.

Change perception so that we can see the emergency.

Don't step on the Indians.

The rhythm continues. At an appropriate time, again judging by the reaction of the public, an actor begins to chant:

If I could turn you on,

If I could drive you out of your wretched mind,

If I could tell you,

I would let you know.*

The actor repeats the chant twice again. The other actors begin then to chant with him. They begin to rise, they continue to chant, they dance, they dance an exultant Indian dance, they dance out into the audience, up the aisles, chanting to the spectators. (Flashout.)

* These are the concluding words of "The Bird of Paradise" by R. D. Laing.

It is the hippies who have risen up from the pavement, rein-
carnations of the American Indian, aspiring to be the Natural
Man as represented by the great Indian culture, the great
suppressed cultures. The culture is assaulted from below.
It is the first step in revolutionary action to change the culture.

The Natural Man confronts the spectator. The Natural Man
knows he can travel without a passport, that he can smoke
marijuana, that he can find ways to live without money, that
he can take off his clothes. He knows how to stop the wars.
That's the flashout.

THE REVOLUTION OF CULTURES

In order to effect a social change, the old values must be
replaced or destroyed and either new values set up or
an open space of no values created for the wind to blow
through. This destruction of old values is The Revolution of Cultures. This is the work of the revolutionary at
this point in the struggle. It is represented here by the
Indians as the Natural Man who serve as examples of
tribal and communitarian alternatives, bringing with
them the gift of beads and the peace-pipe.

The actors have urged the spectators to discard the prohibitions, and to begin to undo the structures which
make these prohibitions. Certain clues have been given
that will be clear to the revolutionary and useful even
to those who have not yet taken revolutionary action.
These clues relate to such subjects as the setting up of
parallel cultures with hints from tribal cultures, the con-

frontation of the social structure with your naked body, the transformation of media, such as the theatre itself, from arenas of imitative action into areas of real action.

The Public must now take the first step.

GUIDES

The I Ching

OF THE RITE OF GUERILLA THEATRE, THE I CHING SAYS:

PROGRESS

```
————————————
————   ————
————————————
————   ————
————   ————
————   ————
```

This hexagram represents the sun rising over the earth. It is the symbol of rapid easy progress which at the same time means ever widening expansion and clarity.

Progress means expansion.

Commentary on the decision:
Progress means making advance. Clarity rises high above the earth.

THE IMAGE (as direction for the actor):

The sun rises over the earth:
The image of Progress.
Thus the superior man himself
Brightens his bright virtue.

The real nature of man is originally good, but it becomes clouded by contact with earthly things and therefore needs purification before it can shine forth in its native clarity.

OF THE VISION OF THE DEATH AND RESURRECTION OF
THE AMERICAN INDIAN, THE I CHING SAYS:

INNER TRUTH

```
————————————
————————————
————    ————
————    ————
————————————
————————————
```

THE JUDGMENT:

Inner Truth. Pigs and Fishes.

Pigs and fishes are the least intelligent of all animals and
therefore the most difficult to influence. In dealing with persons as difficult to influence as a pig or a fish, the whole
secret of success depends on finding the right way of approach. One must first rid oneself of all prejudice and, so
to speak, let the psyche of the other person act without
restraint. Then one will establish contact with him, understand and gain power over him. When a door has thus been
opened, the force of one's personality will influence him, if
in this way one finds no obstacles insurmountable one can
undertake even the most dangerous things and succeed.

THE IMAGE:

Thus the superior man discusses criminal cases
In order to delay executions.
    (The Death and Resurrection of the American Indian)

THE LINES:

If there are secret designs, it is disquieting.
    ("I would let you know.")

I have a good goblet. I will share it with you.
    ("If I could turn you on . . .")

Now he beats the drum, now he stops.

Commentary on the decision:
The yielding are within, yet the strong hold the middle.
Joyous and gentle; thereby truly the country is transformed.

OF THE ACTION LEADING TO THE REVOLUTION
OF CULTURES, THE I CHING SAYS:

THE MARRYING MAIDEN

```
———  ·  ———
———    ———
———————————
———    ———
———————————
———————————
```

Commentary on the Decision:
The Marrying Maiden means the end and the beginning of
humanity.

The Hasidic Rungs

OF THE RUNG OF GOOD AND EVIL,
THE HASIDIM SAY:

"The whole world is a cloak for the lowest rung of holiness,
for its feet, as it were. As it is written: 'And the earth is my
footstool.' "

"In the story of the Creation we read: '. . . and behold, it
was very good.' But, in the passage where Moses reproves
Israel, the verse says: 'See, I have set before thee this day
life and good, and death and evil.' Where did this evil come
from? Evil too is good. It is the lowest rung of perfect good-
ness."

"The Divine Presence comprises all worlds, all creatures,
good and evil. It is true unity. How then can it contain good
and evil, which are self-contradictory? But actually there is
no contradiction, for evil is the throne of good."

"What is needed is not to strike straight at evil but to withdraw to the sources of divine power, and from there to circle
around evil, bend it and transform it into its opposite."

The Colors

Black is beautiful
  is the hidden mystery
  is the gate of the Garden of Eden
  is the path of the unknown
  is the shadow of the murdered Indians falling on the
   culture
  is the shadow that hides the guerilla
  is the color of the sidewalks of New York City and what
   throbs under them
  is the Anarchist flag
  is the Bride of Light
  is the underground

Yoga Preparation I

ASANA YOGA

The object of Yoga: to surpass the limited self.

Four principle forms:

1. Hatha Yoga. Deals with physical principles of the body
   and is divided into two parts:
    a. Asana Yoga: Physical Postures.
    b. Prana Yoga: Physical Breath Control.
2. Raja Yoga: Mental Breath Control. "The obverse of the
   same coin of Hatha Yoga." [Vishnudevananda]
3. Mantra Yoga. Deals with devotion (prayer) and ritual.
4. Laya Yoga. Encompasses the concept of Kundalini and
   the principles of the Chakras.

The three Yoga Preparations indicated on the chart refer:

on Rung I to Asana Yoga
on Rung II to Prana Yoga/Raja Yoga
on Rung III to Mantra Yoga

All forms of Yoga have the same basic prerequisites:

1. Don't injure anything that's alive. Love. (Ahimsa)
2. Tell the truth. Be It. Dig it. (Satya)
3. Keep going. Persist. Whether things are going well or
   not. Whether you feel happy or sad.

4. Simplify.
5. Purify. Body and mind.

Asanas: postures of the body. It is said: the Asanas are as numerous as living beings. The commonest are described and prescribed in Tantric texts. Ritual and magical objects. They form part of a discipline for the conquest of fear. Asana: an aid to clear thought. Asana (postures of the body) produces mental equilibrium. Posture becomes perfect when effort to that end ceases. There are Asanas that you do sitting down, gymnastic Asanas, Asanas done bending. Asanas standing upright, Asanas lying down, or standing on your head. Purpose: to assist in Prana Yoga (breath control) and to help bring on the awakening of Kundalini.

Confrontation

The Culture × Aesthetic Assault

The resistance to The Revolution of Cultures is the culture itself. To penetrate consciousness, to change perception, the actor utilizes Aesthetic Assault.

The Culture:	Aesthetic Assault:
is decadent	is fresh
is idolatrous	is awakening
is hide-bound	is loose-limbed
is arrested	is free
is confused	is clear
is artificial	is art

The Kabbalah

MALKUTH means THE KINGDOM

MALKUTH is THE FEET in the structure of Adam Kadmon.

OF THE SEFIRAH MALKUTH, THE ZOHAR TEACHES:

"There are four lights (Emanations). There is one which sheds light abroad (Chesed/Mercy); one which shines for

itself only (Geburah/Severity); one which gathers light into itself (Tifereth/Beauty); and one which is of itself lightless (Malkuth) which reflects the others as a lamp reflects the sun. To understand this mystery, close thine eye and press thine eyelid and thou wilt discern radiating and luminous colors which can only be seen with closed eyes. The colors thus seen are called luminous because they are not attached to any material background. Just as these can only be seen when the eye is closed, so the higher emanations can only be grasped when the mind completely abstracts itself from the perceptions of sense. The closed eye sees the mirror of light. The open eye sees the mirror which is not luminous. In regard to the lightless mirror the term 'see' is used, but in regard to the luminous mirror the term 'know' is used."
[The Zohar, Book III, 23a–23b]
("Change perception so that we can see the emergency.")

The Zohar identifies the Sefirah Malkuth with the Gate of the Garden of Eden. It is also called the Gate of Tears, of which the Zohar says:

"What can he do since he cannot help it that his heart is heavy? The answer is that 'All gates to heaven have been closed, but the gates of tears have not been closed.' " [Talmud, Berakhot 32b]

"Tears are the expression of sadness and sorrow, and those celestial beings who are appointed over those gates of tears break down all the iron locks and bars and let the tears pass through, so that the entreaties of the grieving suppliants penetrate." [The Zohar, Book IV, 165a]
(The Rite of Guerilla Theatre)

MALKUTH means THE KINGDOM.

The Kingdom which this Sefirah designates is the Material World as Holy Presence. Rung I thus represents the sanctification of the real world.

MALKUTH is THE FEET in the structure of Adam Kadmon.

This represents the presence of the Holy Attributes standing on the earth (his feet on the ground). The first step.

RUNG II
The Rung of Prayer

How
The Rite of Prayer
and
The Vision of the Discovery of the North Pole
lead to
Action II: Bolivia: (In the hills of Bolivia a group of revo-
lutionaries plots its strategy.)
and
THE REVOLUTION OF REVELATION:
The destination must be made clear.

Physical Focus: The Legs

I Ching Oracles: For the Rite: Development (Gradual Progress)
For the Vision: Break-Through (Resoluteness)
For the Action: The Creative

Color: Blue

Yoga Preparation II: Prana Yoga/Raja Yoga (Breathing)

Confrontation: Ignorance × Truth Force

Kabbalistic Sefiroth: Hod (Glory)
Netzach (Triumph)

Rite II
THE RITE OF PRAYER

Without losing the high of his flashout, each actor turns slowly to one of the spectators near him, and, touching him gently, says in a soft voice two words of sanctification. The actor speaks directly to the person. He may speak of a part of his body or his face, a piece of his clothing, or occasionally of one of the objects in the room. Moving through the auditorium quietly, from person to person, the actors praise whatever they come in contact with, and the sound of their voices, their words of praise and of prayer float through the space of the theatre. Holy hand. Holy shirt. Holy smile. Holy teeth. Holy hair. Holy asshole. Holy chair. Holy feet.

It is a prayer of praise. A prayer of the sacredness of all things. It rises gently toward a very quiet ecstasy, ending when the feeling of the prayer, the feeling of universal identification, or oneness, has filled each of us. When the holy relationship has been established. (Flashout.)

Vision II
THE VISION OF THE DISCOVERY
OF THE NORTH POLE

LIGHT: arctic BLUE

The actors are gripped by the cold. The Polar Expedition begins. The explorers struggle toward their goal. As they struggle across the ice they call to each other:

This polar expedition

Took four years to prepare

And will take sixteen months to complete.

It is one of the most difficult

And challenging journeys

Left to be made

By man

On this planet.*

In the center of the playing area the Pole is visible. It spins like a compass at the North Pole. It emits the electromagnetic sound. Configuration: five actors, four directions; the North Pole jutting up from the center, arms extended. As it spins it signals and sends out messages:

Pole of Inaccessibility.

North Pole.

The Revolution does not want power but meaning.

Ice Goddess.

Aurora Borealis.

The Revolution does not want violence but life.

Arctic dust.

Magnetic field.

* These words are taken from the map of the Arctic prepared by the British Trans-Arctic Expedition 1968–69 for the first surface crossing of the Arctic.

The Revolution is based on love.

Ice drift.

Snow density.

After the Revolution there will be no useless work.

North Pole.

Arctic dust.

After the Revolution there will be no money.

Crevasse.

Crystallization.

The Revolution does not want power but meaning.

Wind velocity.

The message draws the others in. They form two corridors of approach through the theatre. Centripetal force pulls them. One by one they tumble toward the Pole, the last coming first, i.e. the actor/explorer at the end of each corridor is assisted by the others on his trip to the Pole, each corridor getting progressively smaller until all the actor/explorers have made the trip and reached their goal. Facing the Pole and spinning with it, they form three radiating spokes, and make signals with their arms.

CONFIGURATION: A revolving wheel sending out messages to the world.

When all the vanguard have made the journey and are part of the large device, the Pole asks The First Question:

WHERE ARE YOU?

Centrifugally propelled, an actor whirls from the Pole and finds a fixed position in clear view of the public and replies:

HERE I AM.

The Pole asks The Second Question:

HOW LONG WILL YOU LIVE?

Another actor whirls out and replies:

IT IS TIME TO REVOLT.

The Pole asks The Third Question:

WHAT DO YOU WANT?

In answer to The Third Question one actor at a time spins off and gives his reply:

To make the world glow with creation.

To make life irresistible.

To feed all the people.

To change the demonic forces into the celestial.

To remove the causes of violence.

To do useful work.

To work for the love of it and not for the money.

To live without the police.

To change myself.

To get rid of the class system.

To re-invent love.

To make each moment creative.

To be free of the force of The State.

To be free to create.

To get rid of a life of material greed.

To free all the energy wasted in financial transaction.

To cut all the bureaucratic wasted time out of life.

To free men from armies.

To stop distorting the mind of the people.

To stop crippling the human body with frustration.

To learn how to breathe.

To live longer than we do.

To be free of the system.

To get rid of central control.

To supply what we need.

To seek what we desire.

To stop wasting the planet.

To stop dying of competition.

To break down the walls that alienate.

To get to know God in His madness.

To make the destination clear.

The final sentences are spoken by the four Directions as they spin off. The last words, "To make the destination clear," are spoken by the Pole. Then the Pole asks:

WHAT IS THIS CALLED?

And with their bodies the actors spell out the word:

ANARCHISM

WHAT IS ANARCHISM?

And with their bodies the actors spell out the word:

PARADISE

and chant the word:

NOW

This is a vision of finding the center, of crystallization, of clarification, of spelling it out, of making the difficult journey in order to find the answer. The center is cold and hard to get to. The center draws us to it. When we reach the center we learn the right answer by being asked the right question. The scene is, in fact, physically difficult to perform. It is the discovery of the axis of the world.

Action II

Bolivia.

How The Rite of Prayer and The Vision of the Discovery of the North Pole lead to The Revolution of Revelation.

In the hills of Bolivia. Moonlight. A group of revolutionaries plots its strategy.

Free theatre. What is to be done?

In the hills of Bolivia a group of revolutionaries meets and discusses The Revolution.

What is The Revolution?

Free theatre. Penetrate the jungle. The mountain. Plan The Revolution.

Play the tin mine. The platinum.

Be the imperialists. Be the exploited.

Be the peasant. And the llama.

Be the American advisors training the counter-revolutionaries.

Be the Americans scouting a new war.

Free theatre. Because in the society we envisage, everyone is free.

Play guerilla warfare. Stop the killing. Die.

Guevara says: "A guerilla wins or dies."

How strong are your legs? Where are they going? How far will they go?

Who is the chairman of this clandestine meeting? Begin.

NOTE:
If the play is being performed on a day on which there has been news of some significant action pertinent to the revolutionary theme of this Rung, the name of the city in which the event took place and references to the event may be substituted for Bolivia.

Example:
In August 1968, when Czechoslovakia was occupied by the Soviet Union, the Text for the Action on this Rung read as follows:

Prague.
How The Rite of Prayer and The Vision of the Discovery of the North

Pole lead to The Revolution of Revelation.
Prague. Free theatre.
Prague. What is to be done?
Prague. What is to be done?
Free theatre. What is to be done?
Prague. What is to be done?
Free theatre. Prague. What is to be done?

Example #2:
In September 1968, during the student demonstrations in Mexico City, the Text of the Action on this Rung read as follows:

Mexico City.
How The Rite of Prayer and The Vision of the Discovery of the North Pole lead to The Revolution of Revelation.
Mexico City. What is to be done?
Free theatre. What is to be done?
Mexico City. What is the answer? What is the question?
Mexico City. Be the army.
Be the students. Be the Rector of the University and resign.
Free theatre. Be the soldiers. Be the generals. Be the dead.
Free theatre. Free theatre where the government controls education.
Free theatre. Free theatre in a city where the C.I.A. functions freely.
Free theatre. What is the problem?
Free theatre. Mexico City. Frankfurt. Madrid. Buenos Aires. Bogota. Tokyo. Prague. What is the goal?
What is to be done?

As the actors speak the lines of the Text, they break up the formation of the letters of the word P A R A D I S E and move to various positions in the theatre.

They then wait at least sixty seconds for the public to initiate the action. If the public begins any sort of enactment or initiates any movement, speech, or dialogue, the actors then join with the spectators in giving support to the scene that the spectators are playing. If this digresses from the revolutionary theme or from the plateau to which we have been brought by the Rite and the Vision, the actors then try to guide the scene back to the meaning of the Rung. If the public is extremely passive and unresponsive, the actors will initiate spontaneous/improvised action. Having initiated an action, they will again wait for the public to take it up.

As the actors work with the public in the Actions, one of the motivating factors of the actor/public relationship is the actors' semi-nudity in confrontation with the spectators' attire. And all its psychological amplifications. As the play progresses, and the involvement and communication between actors and spectators deepen, the psychological balance should reverse. At first the appearance of the actor's body seems strange and the spectator's attire proper. At the end of this contestation it is the spectators' clothing which seems embarrassing and alienating.

The superobjective of the scene is to plan The Non-Violent Anarchist Revolution and to make the meaning and aims of The Revolution clear.

In discussing or enacting the violent aspects of revolution or in discussing or enacting human suffering in all its forms the actor's aim is always to take the scene into the paradisial and hopeful situation. The actors play out with the spectators all the scenes the spectators initiate until the energy suggested by the theme is exhausted. There is no time limit on this scene or on any of the Actions.

Note: At any point in the course of this Action which the actors feel appropriate, they may insert the Text of Phase II.

PHASE II

I want The Revolution that feeds all the starving but doesn't kill anyone.

I want a revolution against all the violence. I start with my own.

I want The Revolution, but I can't encourage killing.

I want The Revolution, but it won't happen unless the people are prepared.

Revolution is change. Revolution means the end of violence. Change the violence into revolution.

When the actors feel that the Action and content of this scene have been consummated, they move on to Rung III.

THE REVOLUTION OF REVELATION

The Revolution of Cultures opens people to new values and ideas.

The Revolution of Revelation describes the aims of The Beautiful Non-Violent Anarchist Revolution. It reveals. It tells what The Revolution is about. It describes another way of being. It creates an atmosphere of Revolution. It speaks of how we can live without money, barter, The State, the police, the armies, and violence. It speaks of a counter-violent strategy. It speaks of what to aim for. It speaks of what to go away from, what to destroy, but, more importantly, of what to create. It makes the destination clear.

GUIDES

The I Ching

OF THE RITE OF PRAYER, THE I CHING SAYS:

DEVELOPMENT (GRADUAL PROGRESS)

———————
———————
——— ———
———————
——— ———
——— ———

THE IMAGE:

On the mountain, a tree.
The image of DEVELOPMENT.
Thus the superior man abides in dignity and virtue,
In order to improve the mores.

The tree on the mountain grows larger slowly and imperceptibly. It spreads and gives shade, and thus through its nature influences its surroundings. Thus it is an example of the active power by which an individual improves the mores of his environment through consistent cultivation of his own moral qualities. The tree on the mountain represents influence by example. The keeping still of the mountain is a symbol for abiding in dignity and virtue. The penetrating attribute of wood (or wind) is a symbol of the positive influence emanating from a good example.

The inexhaustible source of progress is inner calm combined with adaptability to circumstances.

Thus the superior man abides in dignity and virtue in order to improve the mores.

OF THE VISION OF THE DISCOVERY OF THE
NORTH POLE, THE I CHING SAYS:

BREAK-THROUGH (RESOLUTENESS)

——— ———
—————————
—————————
—————————
—————————
—————————

This hexagram signifies a break-through after a long accumulation of tension, as a swollen river breaks through its dikes, or in the manner of a cloudburst. On the other hand, applied to human conditions, it refers to the time when inferior people gradually begin to disappear. As a result of resolute action a change in conditions occurs, a break-through.

THE JUDGMENT:

Break-Through. One must resolutely make the matter known.
It must be announced truthfully.
It is necessary to notify one's own city.
It does not further to resort to arms.

Resolution must be based on a union of strength and friendliness. A compromise with evil is not possible; evil must under all circumstances be openly discredited. The struggle must not be carried on directly by force. If evil is branded, it thinks of weapons, and if we do it the favor of fighting against it blow for blow, we lose in the end because thus we ourselves get entangled in hatred and passion. The best way to fight evil is to make energetic progress in the good.

THE LINES:

There is no skin on his thighs
And walking comes hard.
    ("How strong are your legs?")

In dealing with weeds
Firm resolution is necessary.
Walking in the middle
Remains free of blame.
    ("Where are they going?")

Weeds always grow back again and are difficult to exterminate. So too the struggle against an inferior man in a high position demands firm resolution. One has certain relations with him, hence there is danger that one may give up the struggle as hopeless. But this must not be. One must go on resolutely and not allow himself to be deflected from his course. Only in this way does one remain free of blame.

OF THE ACTION LEADING TO THE REVOLUTION
OF REVELATION, THE I CHING SAYS:

THE CREATIVE

———————
———————
———————
———————
———————
———————

The hexagram includes the power of time and the power of persisting in time, that is, duration.

THE JUDGMENT:

The Creative works sublime success,
Furthering through perseverance.

Another line of speculation goes still further in separating
the words "sublime," "success," "furthering," "perseverance," and parallels them with the four cardinal virtues in
humanity. To sublimity, which as the fundamental principle
embraces all the other attributes, it links love. To the attribute
success are linked the mores, which regulate and organize
the expressions of love and thereby make them successful.
The attribute furthering is correlated with justice, which creates the conditions in which each receives that which accords
with his being, that which is due him and which constitutes
his happiness. The attribute perseverance is correlated with
wisdom, which discerns the immutable laws of all that happens and can therefore bring about enduring conditions.

Time is no longer a hindrance but the means of making
actual what is potential.

Commentary from the Wen Yen on the words of the text:
Succeeding is the coming together of all that is beautiful.
Furtherance is the agreement of all that is just.
Perseverance is the foundation of all action.

The Hasidic Rungs

OF THE RUNG OF PRAYER, THE HASIDIM SAY:

"In every true prayer, it is the community that is praying."

The Colors

Blue is the color men call heavenly
        is the morning light of truth dawning on ignorance
        is the Holy color
        is the current that drives men to the Pole
        is the moonlight shining on the conspirators in the hills
        is the clarity of the destination

is the blood in the veins on the way to the heart
is the cold
is the lament and the magnet
is the in-breath of air

Yoga Preparation II

PRANA YOGA/RAJA YOGA

"Purity of body is necessary if purity of mind is to be gained in its extended Hindu sense. Purification of the Nadis (the physical and astral nerves) is perhaps the chief factor in the preliminary stages of this Yoga; for just as their impurity impedes the ascent of Kundalini, their purity facilitates it. This is the work of Prana Yoga." [Arthur Avalon, "The Serpent Power"]

Prana Yoga: the process by which the ordinary breath is lengthened, strengthened, developed. The principle: mind and breath regulate one another; when the breath is regulated so is the mind. Yoga manuals speak of various ways to inhale, exhale, and retain your breath.

According to the Tantric texts: Kundalini will not awaken until, through proper breath control, enough physical energy (heat) accumulates in the region where she resides to arouse her.

The North Pole asks: "What do you want?" And the reply is given: "To learn how to breathe."

Confrontation

Ignorance × Truth Force

The resistance to The Revolution of Revelation is ignorance. The actor here in confronting the problem, like the Satyagraha of Gandhi, avails himself of the force of truth.

Ignorance: **Truth Force:**
is common   is uncommon

Truth Force is available to all the people.

The Kabbalah

HOD and NETZACH

HOD means GLORY and MAJESTY

HOD is represented by THE LEFT LEG (or the left thigh) in the figure of Adam Kadmon.

NETZACH means TRIUMPH or VICTORY.

NETZACH is represented by THE RIGHT LEG (or the right thigh) in the figure of Adam Kadmon.

OF THE SEFIROTH HOD AND NETZACH,
THE ZOHAR TEACHES:

"From this point he was 'halting on his thigh,' i.e. he attained imperfectly to the conception of 'strength' (Netzach). . . . Thus he restored to its pristine strength that which was weak from the time that Jacob was injured by the guardian angel of Esau. 'He touched the hollow of his thigh.' He derived strength from that which is associated with the attribute of stern justice.

"Netzach is the left thigh. And David came and united it with the right, as it is written: Bliss in the right hand is Netzach. The reason why Jacob's thigh was weak was because the side of impurity touched it and deprived it of its strength. Hence Samuel spoke of the Netzach of Israel, and hence too he spoke always with severity." [The Zohar, Book I, 21b]

"The river that goes forth from Eden to water the garden shall part and become four heads. The first of these is Chesed (Kindness) which is the right arm. From this shall drink Michael and Judah. The second is Geburah (Force) and from it shall drink Gabriel and Dan. The third is Netzach (Victory), the right leg, and from it shall drink Nuriel and Reuben. The fourth is Hod (Majesty), the left leg (referred to in what was said of Jacob, that 'he halted on his left thigh'), and from it shall drink Raphael, whose mission is to heal the ills of the captivity." [The Zohar, Book I, 21b]

Commentary:

This indicates that the performer should allow the spectator to "wound" him in Bolivia (Action II) in order to "heal the ills of the captivity." The direction for the actor is to experience the existing conflict and to make himself susceptible to the public's hostility.

The ladder of the Rungs is the ladder of which Jacob dreamt that leads from earth to heaven; and he dreamt that he wrestled with an angel. And Jacob is wounded in the thigh. Though the performer sanctifies the spectator in The Rite of Prayer (Holy Angel!) and tries to make it crystal clear to him in the North Pole, when they reach Bolivia, they wrestle.

RUNG III
The Rung of Teaching

How
The Rite of Study
and
The Vision of the Creation of Life
lead to
Action III: Here and Now: (There is a group of people
who want to change the
world.)
and
THE REVOLUTION OF GATHERED FORCES

Physical Focus: The Hands

I Ching Oracles: For the Rite: Enthusiasm
For the Vision: Peace
For the Action: Return
(The Turning Point)

Color: Green

Yoga Preparation III: Mantra Yoga

Confrontation: Alienation/Inhibition × Enthusiasm

Kabbalistic Sefiroth: Chesed (Mercy)
Geburah (Severity)

Rite III
THE RITE OF STUDY

LIGHT: WHITE

The actors gather for The Rite of Study. They seat themselves in the center of the playing area, in a spiral form facing inward.

The Rite of Study is a communication that finds its energy source in the actor's center and which transmits itself by means of gestures and phrases that are called Mudras and Mantras.

The Mudras are executed with the arms and hands only. The actors have complete freedom within the form. They can extend their hands and arms above their heads, to the sides, to the floor, in front of them, reaching backwards, they make gestures from the wrists and the fingers, yet every motion must find its source in the center of the actor's body so that all the gestures are always the manifestation of internal impulses. This gives the gesturing actor an appearance related to that of the instructive statuary of India. The actor pays strict attention to the movements of all the actors within his field of vision. Thus the changing forms and rhythms are never totally the individual's but become communications, the Receptive and the Creative. Therefore it is called The Rite of Study.

When the energy generated by the gestures reaches a certain intensity, the actors start to speak the Mantras.

A Mantra is a short phrase or sentence embodying a holy concept. By repeating the phrase or sentence rhythmically it is possible that the essence of the concept begin to enter actively and persuasively the mind of the speaker and hearer.

Each actor speaks when he feels moved to do so. There is no pre-designed order. The actor listens, meditates, studies the Mantras as they are spoken, and answers. He may use one of the Mantras in the text, or invent one. Because of this interchange it is called The Rite of Study.

to be free
is to be free
to eat

to be free
is to be free
of money

to be free
is to be free
to do the work you love

to be free
is to be free
to love

to be free
is to be free
of violence

to be free
is to be free
of property

to be free
is to be
revolutionary

to be free
is to be free
of jails

to be free
is to be free
of police

to be free
is to be free
of the law

to be free
is to be free
of the state

to be free
is to be free
of the system

to be free
is to be free
of prejudice

to be free
is to be free
of hatred

to be free
is to be free
of classes

to be free
is to be free
of stealing

to be free
is to be free
of lies

to be free
is to be free
to feel

to be free
is to be free
to fly

to be free
is to be free
to change

to be free
is to rob death
of its power

to be revolutionary
is to turn
the wheel

At a certain point speech will no longer seem necessary, and the actors stop, each caught in the position of his last Mudra. They are frozen; they have studied; they have not yet reached the point of action. They know this. (Flashout.)

It is possible that at this point the public will freely invent Mantras. The actors hold their positions until the public has finished its inventions.

Slowly the actors rise and begin to move into The Vision of the Creation of Life.

Vision III
THE VISION OF THE CREATION OF LIFE

LIGHT: deep primal GREEN

The actors are rising from their Mudra positions. Their eyes are closed, they move slowly, lifelessly, individually. They are elemental. They are elements before the creation of life. Each one has no connection with any other. As they move with their eyes closed, one performer will touch another by chance. These two now begin to move in a different way. They adhere to each other. They have found a comrade, but not yet a community. Not until five elements have, by chance, come together does the change from the inorganic to the organic take place. The structure is now cellular.

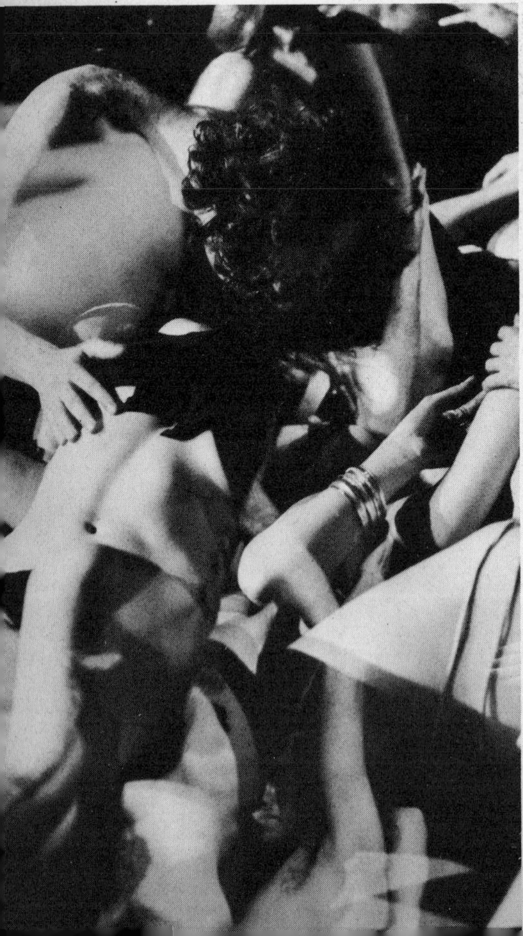

At this point, when five elements have come together, the actors begin to move together as organisms, composed of five actors each. In the playing area now there are several

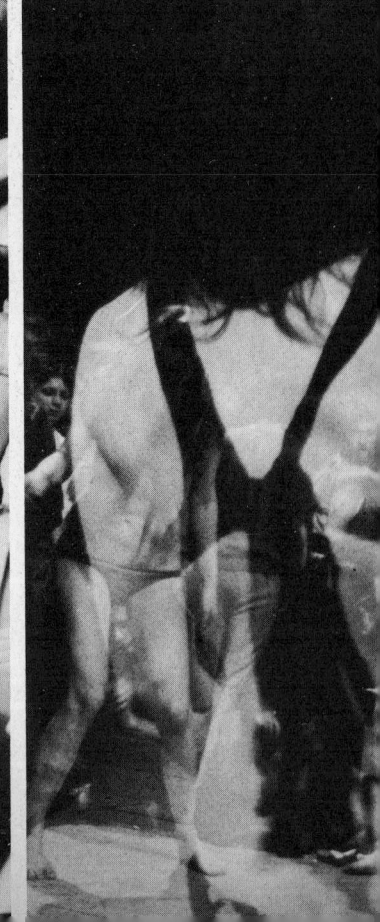

groups. Each group is a primal undersea organism. The actors move always in relation to each other's bodies. Their eyes are now open. They make the sound of the sea and of life until by the presence and movements of one another's bodies they reach an ecstatic state. They rise, stretching their bodies upward, holding each other's hands, lifting their arms up in a circle of five, and make an exultant sound.

IMAGE: Unification as the life-giving force. The elemental structure of the cell as a pattern for social structure.

Action III

This Action takes place in the city in which the play is being performed. On the Chart this Action is designated as taking place in the Here and Now, or, in some cities, the city itself is named on the Chart.

The Text for this scene varies with the location. Information is researched ahead of time on the actual social and political situation in that locality and the Text altered in accordance with what seems appropriate.

The following Text is the Text used at the first performance of the play in Avignon, in July 1968.

Avignon.

How The Rite of Study and The Vision of the Creation of Life lead to The Revolution of Gathered Forces.

How can the City of Avignon be transformed?

Free theatre. Theatre of freedom, of spontaneous joy and action.

Avignon. Free theatre. Imagination takes power.

What actions are the Communists planning?

What tactics are the Anarchists planning?

What are the Gaullists doing?

Be the people in jail in Avignon.

Be the people in the Monoprix.

Be the police in the street.

Be the Pieds Noirs.

Be the Algerians.

The hand can gather.

The hand can write.

The hand can reach.

The hand has five fingers.

A basic cell, says Bakunin, should have five members.

The cell is the basic unit of life. Form cells.

As they speak their lines, or after they speak them, some of the actors leave the playing area to mingle with the public, and some remain in the playing area to speak Phase II.

PHASE II

There are 400 prisoners in the Avignon Jail in the shade of the Palais des Papes. Why are the prisoners there? Who will form a cell to free all men?

Stop the fear.

Stop the repression.

Stop the punishment.

Make it real.

Do it now.

Come up on stage.

Begin.

Who will form a cell to increase the underground press, to make newspapers, leaflets, posters, to tell the people of Avignon what's going on in the world?

Make it real.

Do it now.

Come up on stage.

Begin.

Avignon has a police force of X number of men. Who will form a cell to effect a change of conscience among them?

Avignon has X number of industrial workers and X number of farmers nearby. Who will form cells to tell them about the possibility of another way of living?

In a revolutionary situation who will know how to supply water, electricity, food? Cells are needed to study how to make The Revolution work.

Who will form a cell to disarm the City of Avignon?

The army.

The police.

And the souls of its people.

The following Text was added in New Haven in September 1968:

In the schools, the hospitals, the universities, psychosexual repression is impeding The Revolution. Who dares to form cells to help break down these taboos?

The purpose of this scene is to instigate the gathering of the revolutionary forces.

Discussions are begun on the formation of cells. Radical Action Cells to continue work during and/or after the performance are formed. Posters are printed and all actions initiated by the public are supported by the actors. In order to play this Action with as much awareness of the public's position as possible, the actors should learn as much as possible about the conditions and problems of the area beforehand.

The Action continues as long as its energy is sustained.

THE REVOLUTION OF GATHERED FORCES

After the culture has been altered and perception changed so that we can see the need for revolution and after The Revolution of Revelation in which the meaning of The Revolution has been made clear, people are now ready to gather their forces together and to work together to bring about The Revolution of Action.

The Revolution of Gathered Forces is not theoretical. Its action consists in consolidating that which is already there.

Where the non-violent ambience is feeble, to strengthen, to support, to teach, to arouse.

Where there are revolutionaries working for Non-Violent Revolution, to work with them.

Where The Non-Violent Anarchist Revolution is happening, to support it and to learn from it.

To initiate PRACTICAL WORK.

The work of inspiring the uncommitted, of demystifying those caught in the trap of the political myth continues, of course. The primary function of The Revolution of Gathered Forces is to rally those who are ready and to ready those who are open.

GUIDES

The I Ching

OF THE RITE OF STUDY, THE I CHING SAYS:

ENTHUSIASM

The attribute of the upper trigram is movement; the attributes of the lower are obedience and devotion. This begins a movement that meets with devotion and therefore inspires enthusiasm, carrying all with it. Of great importance, furthermore, is the law of movement along the line of least resistance, which in this hexagram is enunciated as the law for natural events and for human life.

THE JUDGMENT:

Enthusiasm. It furthers one to install helpers.
("Form cells.")

These laws are not external to men but represent the harmony movement immanent in them. It is enthusiasm that enables us to install helpers for the completion of an undertaking without fear or secret opposition. It is enthusiasm, too, that can unify mass movements.

THE IMAGE:

Thunder comes resounding out of the earth:
The image of Enthusiasm.

When at the beginning of summer, thunder—electrical energy—comes rushing forth from the earth again, a prolonged state of tension is resolved. The enthusiasm of the heart expresses itself involuntarily in a burst of song, in dance, and rhythmic movement of the body. From immemorial times the inspiring effect of the invisible sound that moves all hearts and draws them together has mystified mankind.

OF THE VISION OF THE CREATION OF LIFE,
THE I CHING SAYS:

PEACE

The Receptive, which moves downward, stands above; the Creative, which moves upward, is below. Hence their influences meet and are in harmony, so that all living things bloom and prosper. This hexagram belongs to the first month (February–March), at which time the forces of nature prepare the new spring.

THE JUDGMENT:

Peace. The small departs.
The great approaches.

This hexagram denotes a time in nature when heaven seems to be on earth. Heaven has placed itself beneath the earth, and so their powers are in deep harmony. Then peace and blessing descend upon all living things. In the world of man it is a time of social harmony.

In such times when it is possible to extend influence widely, the mind of an able man is set upon going out into life and accomplishing something.

OF THE ACTION LEADING TO THE REVOLUTION OF
GATHERED FORCES, THE I CHING SAYS:

RETURN (THE TURNING POINT)

```
———   ———
———   ———
———   ———
———   ———
———   ———
———————
```

After a time of decay comes the turning point. There is movement but it is not brought about by force. The old is dis-
carded and the new is introduced. Societies of people sharing
the same views are formed. But since these groups come
together in full public knowledge and are in harmony with
the time, all selfish separatist tendencies are excluded, and
no mistake is made.

The Hasidic Rungs

OF THE RUNG OF TEACHING, THE HASIDIM SAY:

"We can learn not only from those whose occupation is to
teach but from every man. Even from a person who is ignorant, or from one who is wicked, you can gain understanding as to how to conduct your life."

" 'You can learn from everything,' the rabbi of Sadagora
once said to his Hasidim. 'Everything can teach us something, and not only everything God has created. What man
has made has also something to teach us.'
    'What can we learn from a train?' one Hasid asked dubi-
        ously.
    'That because of one second one can miss everything.'
    'And from the telegraph?'
    'That every word is counted and charged.'
    'And from the telephone?'
    'That what we say here is heard there.' "

The Colors

Green is the fruitful
       is the growth as in plants and study
       is the chlorophyll that renders light into life
       is the color of the here and now
       is the grass-roots of the gathered forces
       is the sea and the land where life emerges
       is new
       is the fertile gesture
       is the jungle and the oasis
       is the signal to go

Yoga Preparation III

MANTRA YOGA

Mantra Yoga comprises all the ways in which the mind is controlled by the things it observes—the manifold objects of the world of name and form. The mind itself is modified by what it perceives. Contemplation, then, of what is sought is an active form of Mantra. The practice of Mantra is rooted in sound, the ceremonial repetition and contemplation of concepts leading to the freeing of worldly energy so that it may pursue its spiritual voyage. This means liberating Kundalini. The practice of Mantra Yoga is the basic principle of The Rite of Study.

Confrontation

Alienation/Inhibition × Enthusiasm

The resistance to The Revolution of Gathered Forces is alienation or inhibition. To transform this obstacle to the work, the actor arouses enthusiasm. (Compare I Ching Oracle for The Rite of Study.)

Alienation/Inhibition:	Enthusiasm:
is isolation	is social
separates	mingles
is competitive	is collective
is withdrawn	is friendly
is down	is high
is repressing	is liberating
is deadly	is lively
is saying I	is saying We

The Kabbalah

CHESED and GEBURAH

CHESED means MERCY, KINDNESS, GRACE.

CHESED is associated with light, the source of blessing.

GEBURAH means JUSTICE, FORCE, RIGOR, SEVERITY.

GEBURAH is associated with darkness, the source of chastisement.

CHESED and GEBURAH are THE HANDS (or the arms) in the figure of Adam Kadmon.

OF THE SEFIROTH CHESED AND GEBURAH,
THE ZOHAR TEACHES:

"Our object is to awaken Mercy (Chesed) and to bring about the subjugation of the Masters of Severity (Geburah) so that they shall be impotent." [The Zohar, Book V, 149a]

Commentary:
The difficult balance between Justice and Mercy, between Kindness and Strictness is one of the central themes of the Zohar. The desire of the pious is to create an unbalance in which Mercy tempers Justice, and this teaching the Zohar refers to as a great mystery and as its "hidden" message. This is also the Apokatastasis of which "Paradise Now" speaks, and here in The Rite of Study this mystery is revealed as in the following image from the Zohar in which we take the "blowing of the trumpets" to be the recitations of the Mantras and the Mudric gestures of the Rite.

"At the time when Rigor (Geburah) impends over the world there are deposited ever so many records, notes and books so that nothing is forgotten. Many are the executioners who bestir themselves on that day to take part in the world's judgment. Israel on that day blows the trumpet and the Holy One, blessed be He, takes compassion on them and changes Rigor into Mercy. Hence whoever blows the trumpet should know the root of the matter, so as to concentrate his mind on the meaning of the blowing and to perform it with understanding." [The Zohar, Book V, 149b]

Relating to the formation of cells (The Vision of the Creation of Life), the Zohar says:

"It is written, 'and he meteth out waters by measure,' implying that God literally measured them out so that they were for the well-being of the world when they came from the side of Geburah (Force). Rabbi Abba said: 'When the scholars of old came to this place, they used to say: "The lips of the wise move but they say nothing lest they bring down punishment on themselves." ' " [The Zohar, Book I, 32b]

Commentary:
"Punishment," because they were expounding a dangerous doctrine: The victory of Mercy over Justice. In the "measuring out of the waters," as in the formation of cells, the limitation is stressed because it prevents "Power."

Of the hands, the Zohar says:
"Sometimes when all agree to condemn there comes the right hand which is outstretched to receive those that repent; this is the Shekinah (Divine Presence) which is called 'right hand' from the side of Chesed (Kindness). This hand saves from punishment." [The Zohar, Book I, 22b–23a]

Commentary:
"Stop the punishment. Stop the repression." The actor can choose to play from the right hand of gentleness, or he can play the scene from the force of his left hand, or he can play the polarity, or he can play the merciful hand and let the public play the severity, or vice versa.

RUNG IV
The Rung
of the Way

How
The Rite of Universal Intercourse
and
The Vision of Apokatastasis
lead to
Action IV: Jerusalem: (There is a group of victims who
have become victors and are now
becoming executioners. What do
the pacifists do?)
and
THE EXORCISM OF VIOLENCE and THE SEXUAL
REVOLUTION

Physical Focus: The Genitals

I Ching Oracles: For the Rite: Contemplation (View)
For the Vision: Obstruction
For the Action: Opposition

Color: Red

Chakra: Muladhara (The Root Chakra)

Confrontation: Hostility × Love Force

Kabbalistic Sefirah: Yesod (Foundation)

Rite IV
THE RITE OF UNIVERSAL
INTERCOURSE

LIGHT: WHITE

The actors gather near the center of the playing area. They lie down together on the stage floor, embracing. Their bodies form a pile, caressing, moving, undulating, loving. They are breaking the touch barrier. Each performer reaches out to the performers who are around him. He touches, caresses, moves toward any or all of the other actors. There is no choosing or discrimination. All the bodies are beautiful. They reach out toward one another. The actors make a low humming sound. If a member of the public joins this group, he is welcomed into the Rite.

If two actors should feel closely drawn toward each other, they separate themselves from the group and seat themselves alongside it in the position which in India is named Maithuna. It consists of a male and a female position, though in The Rite of Universal Intercourse a person of either sex may assume either position. The person in the male position sits cross-legged on the floor. The person in the female position sits facing him, resting on his thighs, legs coiled around his hips, arms resting on his shoulders, the organs of sex in contact. It is a form of deep physical absorption and communication. After a while the couples return to the group. Anyone may return to the Maithuna position again if he wants to. And with anyone with whom he or she wishes. The Rite lasts fifteen minutes.

Sensation and pleasure are aroused in the genital organs and in the erotic chambers of the mind. Body contact without game-playing. The Rite of Prayer, expression of the holiness of all things, is expanded here. Spiritual understanding unifies with physical experience. (Flashout.)

Vision IV
THE VISION OF APOKATASTASIS

LIGHT: RED

The actors rise from The Rite of Universal Intercourse and take positions in pairs, a victim and an executioner. The executioner stands with his back to the audience, his right hand extended toward the head of the victim, his fingers pointing in the children's-game representation of a gun. The victim stands with his hands behind his back facing the audience. The position is as close an approximation as possible of the photograph taken by Edward Adams which appeared in the newspapers in January 1968 showing the execution of a captured Vietcong by the Chief of the Saigon Police. The executioners in unison make the sound of the firing of a gun. The victims fall simultaneously. The victims rise again and resume their original positions; the executioners fire, the victims fall. The victims rise, the executioners fire, the victims fall. This is repeated twenty times. At the end of twenty enactments of this repeated dream, the victims begin to address the executioners with the words of The Rite of Prayer: Holy Eyes, Holy Legs, Holy Mouth. . . . And the executioners reply with the phrases of The Rite of Guerilla Theatre: I Am Not Allowed To Take My Clothes Off, You Can't Live If You Don't Have Money, I Am Not Allowed To Smoke Marijuana, I Don't Know How To Stop The Wars, I Am Not Allowed To Travel Without A Passport. The executioners continue to fire, the victims to rise, the victims to use the words of The Rite of Prayer, the executioners to speak the words of The Rite of Guerilla Theatre, until the executioners are moved to re-

spond, not with violence, but with love, and gently address the victims with the words of The Rite of Prayer. The Vision ends with the embrace of victim and executioner. (Flashout.)

If a member of the public should, in the course of the Vision, intercede or attempt to intercede in the execution, the executioner continues his action saying to the peacemaker the words of The Rite of Guerilla Theatre until he is convinced or persuaded by the spectator/participant to stop. He then addresses the words of The Rite of Prayer to him and includes him in the embrace. (Flashout.)

It is the vision of APOKATASTASIS, the reversal, the turning of the demonic forces, the transformation of the demonic forces into the celestial.

Though the techniques of peacemaking remain a mystery to everyone, such clues as we have are given here; that is, that the opponent must be approached with high regard and tenderness and that the opponent's painful motives must be taken into consideration. Clue from the teachers: Gandhi: AHIMSA: without hurting: Love Force.

It is a recurrent dream, stuck somewhere in the collective unconscious, which resolves joyously through the persistence of counter-violent action.

Lenin points out that The Revolution will have to take place with human nature remaining unchanged. But this is the Rung on the ladder on which the turning point has been reached at which it will be possible to bring about change without violence. Revolution without violence. How can this be? This is the subject of all our research and work.

Historical conditions change. Apokatastasis. Revolution without violence. Human nature changes. The demonic forces meet a greater force. (Flashout.)

NOTE

From the international edition of the "Herald Tribune" of December 6, 1967:

New York, Dec. 5.—The police tussled for five hours with more than 1,000 anti-war demonstrators today and arrested 264.

Dr. Benjamin Spock, the baby doctor and pacifist, and Allen Ginsberg, the poet, were among the first to be taken into custody. . . .

Poetical Politics

Just before he was led away, Mr. Ginsberg burst forth poetically:

> "Pentagon, Pentagon,
> Reverse consciousness,
> Apokatastasis."

He explained to some confused companions that the last word meant "a transformation of satanic forces into celestial."

Action IV

Jerusalem.

How The Rite of Universal Intercourse and The Vision of Apokatastasis lead to The Exorcism of Violence and The Sexual Revolution.

Apokatastasis. The transformation of the demonic forces into the celestial.

Free theatre. With body and voice, inhibition and exhibition, we tell each other where we are at.

Free sexual theatre. Free action.

Break the touch barrier.

Be the Israeli women with guns.

Be the repressed Arab women.

Be the Arab and Jewish fanatics.

Find a way to reverse history.

Who are the victims? Who are the executioners? What do you choose?

Fuck the Jews.

Fuck the Arabs.

Fuck means peace.

Fuck means peace.

The actors wait. Free theatre. The intent of Free Theatre is to allow the public and the actors to do whatever they want. Sometimes the actors serve as guides. In enacting the prob-

lem of Arab-Jewish hostility, the separation between men, and the artificial barriers that increase violence and suffering, the actor/guides seek to consummate the action by a sexual unification. They lead the public back into The Rite of Universal Intercourse so that Action IV always ends with

The Rite of Universal Intercourse, this time the actor/guides encouraging the participation of the public. In The Rite of Universal Intercourse the division between actor and public diminishes. This diminution of the division between actor and spectator becomes an image for the disappearance of the division between Arab and Jew. And all its counterparts.

THE EXORCISM OF VIOLENCE AND THE SEXUAL REVOLUTION

The fundamental taboo that is channeled into violence is the sexual taboo. To overcome violence we have to overcome the sexual taboo.

The work of liberation from sexual repression must be a parallel of all revolutionary work and must take place during all revolutionary stages. But there comes a point at which no further progress can be made without abolishing standards that cripple the natural man sexually, and this point comes precisely when we confront the fundamental problem of violence.

The Beautiful Non-Violent Anarchist Revolution will only take place after The Sexual Revolution because before that the energy is violent.

GUIDES

The I Ching

OF THE RITE OF UNIVERSAL INTERCOURSE,
THE I CHING SAYS:

CONTEMPLATION (VIEW)

This hexagram has a double meaning: it means both contemplation and being seen, in the sense of being an example.

The meaning of the hexagram of Approach and Contemplation is that they partly give and partly take. The lower trigram is devoted, the upper is gentle. (Maithuna)

THE JUDGMENT:

Contemplation.
Full of trust they look up to him.

A great view is above. Devoted and gentle. Central and correct, something for the world to view. Those below look and are transformed. He affords them a view of the divine way of heaven, and the whole world submits.

OF THE VISION OF APOKATASTASIS,
THE I CHING SAYS:

OBSTRUCTION

Obstruction means difficulty. This hexagram represents obstructions that appear in the course of time but that can and should be overcome. This requires the will to persevere. This unswerving inner purpose brings good fortune in the end.

THE LINES:

In the midst of the greatest obstructions,
Friends come.

Here we see a man who is called to help in an emergency. He should not seek to evade the obstructions, no matter how dangerously they pile up before him. The power of his spirit is strong enough to attract helpers whom he can efficiently organize, so that through the well-directed cooperation of all participants the obstruction is overcome.

OF THE ACTION LEADING TO THE EXORCISM OF
VIOLENCE AND THE SEXUAL REVOLUTION,
THE I CHING SAYS:

OPPOSITION

———————————
———— ————
———————————
———— ————
———————————

This hexagram is composed of the trigrams Li above, i.e., flame, which burns upward, and Tui below, i.e., the lake, which seeps downward. These two movements are in direct contrast. Furthermore, Li is the second daughter and Tui the youngest daughter, and although they live in the same house they belong to different men; hence their wills are not the same but are divergently directed.

THE LINES:

Isolated through opposition,
One sees one's companion as a pig covered with dirt,
As a wagon full of devils.
First one draws a bow against him,
Then one lays the bow aside.
He is not a robber; he will woo at the right time.
As one goes, rain falls; then good fortune comes.

Here the isolation is due to misunderstanding; it is brought about not by outer circumstances but by inner conditions. A man misjudges his best friends, taking them to be unclean as a dirty pig and as dangerous as a wagon full of devils. He adopts an attitude of defense. But in the end, realizing his mistake, he lays the bow aside, perceiving that the other is approaching with the best of intentions for the purpose of close union. Thus the tension is relieved. The union resolves the tension, just as falling rain relieves the sultriness preceding a thunderstorm.

The Hasidic Rungs

OF THE RUNG OF THE WAY, THE HASIDIM SAY:

"Everyone should have pity upon his body and allow it to share in all that illumines the soul. We must purify the body very greatly so that it may share in everything the soul receives, so that there may be a change in the present state where the soul attains to lofty matters and the body knows nothing about them. But if the body is given a share, it can also be of use to the soul. For, at times, the soul falls from its rung, and then the purified body can help it up again through the power of the light it has absorbed. That is why Job says: 'From out my flesh shall I see God.' "

The Colors

Red is the blood
     is the name of the radical activist
     is the fire created by union
     is the poppy and the rose
     is the eye of love
     is the sacrificial altar of Jerusalem
     is the hostility and the love that overcomes it
     is the hot phallus
     is the banner of the community of comrades
     is the revolution

The Chakras

THE MULADHARA CHAKRA

"Now we come to the Muladhara Chakra. It is placed below the genitals and above the anus. Here dwells Kundalini, the carrier of revelation. Inside is Shiva (Consciousness) in his phallic form. He is revealed by Knowledge and Meditation. Like a sleeping snake, Kundalini lies coiled around him. By her radiance it is that the whole of this Universe and this Cauldron is illumined. By meditation on her, a man becomes Lord of Speech and an adept in all kinds of learning and his inmost spirit becomes full of gladness." [The Sat-Chakra-Nirupana of Sri Purnanandayati]

"It is for the creation of all the worlds that Kundalini uncoils. . . . The object of Kundalini-Yoga is to raise Consciousness to its perfect expression . . . whereby man exchanges his limited experience for that which is the unlimited Whole or Perfect Bliss." [Arthur Avalon, "The Serpent Power"]

Commentary:
The Kundalini Power is the Sexual Energy, not only in its gross form, but awake, that is, in a state of conscious awareness. The release of the Sexual Energy from her inactive dormant state leads to that fulfillment which is here called Perfect Bliss or Peace. ("Fuck means Peace.")

The Rite of Universal Intercourse is the spiritual awakening of Kundalini. In the Tantra Mythology this leads to the union (Maithuna) of Kundalini with Shiva. On the physical plane Maithuna denotes sexual union.

The uncoiling of Kundalini (the result of Meditation, Prayer, Devotion, Ritual, Physical Exercise and Purification, Breath Control, Knowledge, and Action) means breaking the touch barrier, physically, sexually, and spiritually.

Both the Zohar and the sacred Hindu texts place the transforming element in the sexual region and relate the beginning of the highest wisdom to the generative organs. Thus in both these cultures the center of sexual energy is referred to as the Foundation.

Apokatastasis: The transformation of the demonic forces into the celestial: the voyage of Kundalini from the Earth Center (The Muladhara Chakra) to the domain of Supreme Bliss (The Sahasrara Chakra, the seventh Chakra).

Confrontation

Hostility   × Love Force
  (resulting from an
  unsatisfactory life)

The resistance to The Exorcism of Violence and The Sexual Revolution rises from the hostility that is the result of an unsatisfactory life. The actor meets this hostility by summoning the Love Force.

Hostility:	Love Force:
disintegrates	magnetizes
dehumanizes	promotes evolution
kills	speaks
is anti-sexual	is irresistible
negates	flowers

The Love Force, Ahimsa, meaning "without hurting." Gandhi's prerequisite for Non-Violent Action.

The Kabbalah

YESOD

YESOD means FOUNDATION

In the figure of Adam Kadmon the FOUNDATION is set in the region of THE REPRODUCTIVE ORGANS.

In the Zohar the Sefirah Yesod is called Zaddik, or "The Righteous" because it is associated with the sign of the Covenant (the Circumcision).

OF THE SEFIRAH YESOD, THE ZOHAR TEACHES:

" 'and God said, Let the earth put forth grass, herb yielding seed, and fruit trees bearing fruit after its kind.' By 'fruit tree' is meant the Tree of Knowledge of Good and Evil which puts forth blossoms and fruit. 'Bearing fruit' is the Zaddik, the basis (Foundation) of the world. 'After its kind' means

that all human beings who have in them the spirit of holiness
which is the blossom of that tree are stamped as being of
its kind. This stamp is the covenant of holiness, the covenant
of peace.'' [The Zohar, Book I, 33a]

Commentary:
This generative power, which is here described as fruitful-
ness, is the confluence of the sexual and the spiritual. On
the Rungs of "Paradise Now" it is enacted in The Rite of Universal Intercourse. In the Zohar this grade leads to the Tree
of Knowledge of Good and Evil, which is that division into the
celestial and demonic which Apokatastasis seeks to transform.

By "all human beings who have in them the spirit of holiness" the Kabbalists refer to that "Exorcism of Violence and
The Sexual Revolution" which will bring about the unification of the divided Jerusalem.

RUNG V
The Rung
of Redemption

How
The Rite of the Mysterious Voyage
and
The Vision of the Integration of the Races
lead to
Action V: Paris: (Time Future: The Non-Violent Anarch-
ist Revolution)
and
THE REVOLUTION OF ACTION:
The plan goes into effect: burn the money!

Physical Focus: The Abdomen (The Stomach)

I Ching Oracles: For the Rite: Deliverance
For the Vision: Following
For the Action: Revolution (Molting)

Color: Orange

Chakras: Svadhisthana and Manipura

Confrontation: Rigidity × Movement

Kabbalistic Sefirah: Tifereth (as The Essence)

Rite V
THE RITE OF THE MYSTERIOUS VOYAGE

LIGHT: WHITE

The Rite of the Mysterious Voyage is about the relationship of the individual to the community and of the community to the individual.

From out of the sound that is being made by those performing The Rite of Universal Intercourse comes another sound. It is made by the actor who is beginning The Rite of the Mysterious Voyage. The other actors, hearing this sound—and it is a disturbing sound—disperse and form a circle around the Mysterious Voyager. The Voyager flips out. He allows himself to be possessed by whatever demonic forces are available to him. The community helps him take his trip. They watch him intently but neither coax him nor hinder him. The community becomes involved in the essence of his trip. They follow his changes. They do not seek to soothe him, nor to bring him back from where he is, but urge him to go further in the direction in which he is going. In this way they support him, and by the support of sharing his changes, they give him the courage to take the trip, so that his solo trip becomes possible through the support of the community.

The Voyager abandons himself to the impulses of the forces that possess him; his body makes the sounds and gestures that rise out of his internal experience. It is a form of trance, self-induced. Trance takes the Voyager into the unknown. He expresses his pain. He does not suppress. Nor does the community repress his impulses, but rather gives him energy that takes him further. The guiding principle of the Rite is that if the Voyager does not withdraw, but wrestles with the hostile and demonic within himself, going into the darker recesses of his mind, he will return from the trip recharged, purified, reinforced by virtue of the help the community gives him. It is the exorcism of fear. At the completion of the trip both Voyager and Community reach a highly positively-charged state. (Flashout.)

Vision V
THE VISION OF THE INTEGRATION
OF THE RACES

LIGHT: ORANGE

The actors mingle in the middle of the playing area. They exchange hostile looks. Everyone stops. The actors divide into opposing camps. The dream is based on reality.

One of the actors turns to another and says:

JEW.

The Jewish actor responds with the word:

CHRISTIAN.

They speak these words quietly but with deep hosility. Contemptuously. The two actors look at each other for a moment, then turn and move quickly to opposite sides of the playing area. All the actors go through the same process until all the actors in the playing area stand in two opposing camps. They then move slowly toward each other, again exchanging hostile looks and moving in a manner to represent suppressed violence. When they reach the center of the stage, they mingle and everyone stops. An actor says sharply to another:

BLACK.

The black actor responds:

WHITE.

The actors divide into two opposing camps.

Again they regard each other hostilely, mingle, stop. An actor calls another actor

YOUNG.

The young actor replies:

OLD.

The actors separate into two opposing camps. They approach, mingle, stop. An actor calls another actor

SHORT.

The short actor replies:

TALL.

The actors separate into two opposing camps. They approach, mingle, stop. They turn toward the public. Slowly, hostilely, they move toward the public. They address the public individually and as individuals.

At first they use the words of the opening part of the Vision: BLACK WHITE JEW CHRISTIAN OLD SHORT TALL YOUNG. Then they include other words, at first more or less appropriate, then more imaginative, often moving into the realm of absurdity. Under the influence of the humor the tone

changes from anger to friendliness, from hatred to affection.
Once outside of the area of hostility, the actors go one step
further, from the absurd to the profound, saying

I/THOU

to the spectators. (Flashout.)

The flashout comes from the moment of communication between the actor and the spectator when the actor feels a
response from his communication of the words

I/THOU

Action V

Paris.

How The Rite of the Mysterious Voyage and The Vision of the Integration of the Races lead to The Revolution of Action.

Free theatre. Take action.

Paris. Time future. The Non-Violent Anarchist Revolution.

Paris. The day we stop using money.

What are the police doing?

What does the President of the French Republic do?

What are the workers doing?

How does it feel to burn the money?

How do you enact the fall of The State?

What are the Marxists doing?

Who cleans the sewers?

Play the re-occupation of the Odeon. Re-occupy the factories.

Abandon the university.

Let loose the creative disorder.

Feed all the people.

Play the turning.

Play the joy.

Play the end of useless labor.

The Revolution of Action is the turning point between the period of preparatory work and the period of active social restructure. Therefore the play from this point on is a projec-

tion into time future. Now the play examines what happens after The Revolution of Cultures is already underway, after the destination has been made clear, after the forces have been gathered, after The Sexual Revolution and The Exorcism of Violence. Now we begin. It is the work of the actors to guide the public into a projection of the revolutionary situation.

THE REVOLUTION OF ACTION

The Non-Violent Anarchist Revolution is the change effected by the production and distribution of all that people need without the use of coercive bribery, violence, or hated labor. It means an attempt to live together without punitive law, jails, police, armies, and the control which money exercises on work, production, and the human character. Therefore it cannot be the change imposed by a new ruling class. The Anarchists believe that it is possible to feed all the people and to solve all the problems of the human condition better without a money incentive, without rules implying that if you don't work you don't eat, and without the patterns of living imposed by political and economic systems. The Anarchists believe that all men can do the work they want to do and can live peacefully and creatively together because the human mind that has invented the intricate system of production-by-means-of-exploitation and the regulation of consumption-by-means-of-want-and-overproduction will invent ways to feed all the people without the use of violence and coercive measures. Get rid of the money system, says the Anarchist, get rid of central governmental control, and what will happen?

Other incentives will be found. Money puts The State in the position of central control. The hierarchy of money and state can be broken if people could find a way to do without money. Therefore The Revolution of Action is that period during which a significant number of people begin to function without the money system. No barter, no exchange. What is needed can be made and distributed without payment of any sort.

The Revolution can then create situations which by virtue of their examples will win people over.

If there is no law and no government control, says the Anarchist, what will happen? The Revolution is predicated on both individual and collective change, and this question cannot be answered adequately if we imagine this exterior change in the structure of society without a parallel change in human character.

GUIDES

The I Ching

OF THE RITE OF THE MYSTERIOUS VOYAGE,
THE I CHING SAYS:

DELIVERANCE

—— ——
—— ——
————————
—— ——
————————
—— ——

Here the movement goes out of the sphere of danger. The obstacle has been removed; the difficulties are being resolved. Deliverance is not yet achieved; it is just in its beginning, and the hexagram represents its various stages.

These periods of sudden change have great importance. Just as rain relieves atmospheric tension, making all the buds burst open, so a time of deliverance from burdensome pressure has a liberating effect on life.

Deliverance means release from tension.

OF THE VISION OF THE INTEGRATION OF THE RACES,
THE I CHING SAYS:

FOLLOWING

—— ——
—————
—————
—— ——
—— ——
—————

THE LINES:

The standard is changing.

We must not associate exclusively with people who share our views or with members of our own party; instead we must go out and mingle freely with all sorts of people, friends or foes. That is the only way to achieve something.

Following tolerates no old prejudices. Followers readily join in a movement that is associated with joyousness.

OF THE ACTION LEADING TO THE REVOLUTION OF
ACTION, THE I CHING SAYS:

REVOLUTION (MOLTING)

—— ——
—————
—————
—————
—— ——
—————

The Chinese character for this hexagram means in its original sense an animal's pelt, which is changed in the course of the years by molting. From this word is carried over the moltings in political life, the great revolutions.

Political revolutions are extremely grave matters.

The time of revolution is truly great.

First, one must be able to await the right moment. Second, one must proceed the right way so that one will have the sympathy of the people and so that excesses will be avoided. Third, one must be correct and entirely free of all selfish motives. Fourth, the change must answer a real need.

The Hasidic Rungs

OF THE RUNG OF REDEMPTION, THE HASIDIM SAY:

"Everyone should know and consider the fact that he, in the particular way he is made, is unique in the world, and that no one like him has ever been. For if someone like him had already been there would be no reason for him to be in this world. Actually, everyone is something new in this world, and here he must perfect his particular being, for because he is still imperfect the coming of the Messiah is delayed."

"A man cannot find redemption until he sees the flaws in his soul, and tries to efface them. Nor can a people be redeemed until it sees the flaws in its soul and tries to efface them. But whether it be a man or a people, whoever shuts out the realization of his flaws is shutting out redemption. We can be redeemed only to the extent to which we see ourselves."

"In free space there is neither right nor left. In the same way, there is reward and punishment only in this, and not in the Messianic world."

The Colors

Orange is the color of the love apple
            is the color of the integrated races
            is the movement that sways rigidity
            is the integration of red and yellow

is the color of the flames that burn the money
is the gong that announces the action
is the juice, pulp, taste, and nourishment
is the lighting of the lamps
is the sunset, the sunrise, the gunfire
is sensuous

The Chakras

THE SVADHISTHANA CHAKRA

"He who meditates upon this stainless Lotus (Chakra) is freed immediately from all his enemies." [The Sat-Chakra-Nirupana]

"(this verse refers to) the six evil inclinations: Lust, Anger, Greed, Disinclination, Pride, Envy." [Arthur Avalon, "The Serpent Power"]

The Hamsopanishad assigns these Qualities to this Chakra: Credulity, Suspicion, Disdain, Disinclination, False Knowledge, Pitilessness.

"It is noteworthy that the Qualities of the two lower Chakras (The Svadhisthana and The Manipura) are all bad: those of the Anahata Chakra are mixed, those of the Lalana Chakra are predominately good, and those of the Soma Chakra wholly so; thus indicative of an advance as we proceed from the lower to the higher centres, and this must be so as the individual approaches or lives in his higher principles. That they (the "bad" Qualities) exist at any particular Chakra is said to be shown by their disappearance when Kundalini ascends through the Chakra. Thus the bad Qualities of the lower Chakras pass away in the Yogi who raises Kundalini above them." [Arthur Avalon, "The Serpent Power"]

Commentary:
The process of transforming the six enemies relates both to The Rite of the Mysterious Voyage and to The Vision of the Integration of the Races.

In the Svadhisthana Chakra resides stimulation in the sense of taste. The Manipura Chakra which also influences Rung V is located in the abdomen, or spinal region of the navel. These two elements, including the knowledge that as Kundalini passes through she dissolves, or pacifies, stimulation of taste refers to the principle inherent in the cry: "Feed all the people."

The pacification of greed is essential to the realization of The Revolution of Action, in which the monetary system is dissolved and with it the sense of private property.

THE MANIPURA CHAKRA

Note: The influence of the Manipura Chakra, as it relates to the Chart, affects both Rung V and Rung VI.

"By meditating on this Navel Lotus the power to destroy and create the world is acquired." [The Sat-Chakra-Nirupana] ("Let loose the creative disorder.")

Confrontation

Rigidity × Movement

The resistance to The Revolution of Action is rigidity, and the actor finds its physical opposite in movement, its mental opposite in flexibility.

Rigidity:	**Movement:**
won't let go	explores
is brittle	stirs up the dust
is severe	flows into and around things
is frightened	is adventurous
is paralyzing	is changing

The Kabbalah

TIFERETH

TIFERETH means ESSENCE.

In the Zohar this Sefirah is designated as:
1. The Body of Israel and 2. The Beauty of Israel.

OF THE SEFIRAH TIFERETH AS THE BODY OF ISRAEL
(THE ABDOMEN), THE ZOHAR TEACHES:

"It is written: 'A river went forth from Eden.' [Genesis II: 10]
And the name of that river is called Life, because Life issues
thence to the world. The great and mighty tree which is food
for all is called the Tree of Life (Tifereth) because its roots
are in that life. We have learnt that that river sends forth
deep streams to water the Garden (Paradise) and to feed the
trees and shoots. Hence they flow further till they are all
gathered into the place called Sea, which is the Sea of Wisdom. All who are fed below are fed from this place, as it is
written: 'The eyes of all wait on thee and thou givest them
their meat in due season.' [Psalms CXLIV, 15]" [The Zohar,
Book V, 58a]

Commentary:
The Zohar refers to this Sefirah as the Tree of Life. The image
of the River called Life refers to the Mysterious Voyage.

Tifereth is the Essence because it is related to the line "Feed
all the people." In the structure of Adam Kadmon, TIFERETH
is both THE STOMACH and THE HEART. Thus the feeding of
which the Zohar speaks is both the food of the stomach and
of the spirit.

Tifereth is also called the Central Pillar which unites the
Right and the Left. The actor can take this as direction for
the playing of The Integration of the Races, in which he (the
actor) plays the Central Column, turning the divided seg-
ments toward one another, using himself as a pivot on
which the turning takes place.

RUNG VI
The Rung of Love

How
The Rite of Opposite Forces
and
The Vision of the Magic Love Zap
         of the Non-Violent Conquest of the Pentagon
lead to
Action VI: Capetown/Birmingham: (The Blacks are con-
                              fronting the Whites with
                              revolution. How do they
                              overcome?)
and
THE REVOLUTION OF TRANSFORMATION:
The Struggle Period

Physical Focus: The Heart

I Ching Oracles: For the Rite: The Caldron
                 For the Vision: Before Completion
                 For the Action: Peace

Color: Yellow

Chakras: Manipura and Anahata

Confrontation: Fear × Energetic Action

Kabbalistic Sefirah: Tifereth (as Beauty)

Rite VI
THE RITE OF OPPOSITE FORCES

LIGHT: WHITE

When The Revolution of Action has reached its culmination, an actor lies down in the center of the playing area. He is the Subject of the Rite. He relaxes his mind and body. His body is limp. His mind is open and in free space. He makes a loud steady sound. He breathes deeply and fully. The other actors form a wide circle around him.

Singly or in groups the actors approach the Subject. They can do anything they want with his body.

They bring to bear upon his body, through the medium of a variety of physical assaults, the positive and negative charges of both disturbing and soothing forces. They seek both to distract his concentration and to strengthen it. They stop at nothing in their attempts with both physical movement and sound to reach the depths of his physical being. The Subject adheres to his center, and the sound which emanates from his center never falters.

By accepting the forces that come at him, by maintaining his center, by maintaining his passive state, the Subject becomes the Receptive; and all of the energy released toward him charges him and takes him on a trip which finally releases him into a state of transcendent energy and transformation. (Flashout.)

The Subject rises and signals. It is the signal of his here and now.

Vision VI
THE VISION OF THE MAGIC LOVE ZAP

LIGHT: YELLOW (GOLD)

The actors form a pentagon. Within the pentagon is a formation representing a large statue of Mammon made by five
actors. At the foot of the statue is an actor, spread-eagled
on the floor, in the position of a victim about to be sacrificed.

Behind the statue or altar are four priests. The actors who compose the five walls of the pentagon assume the fierce attitudes of the stone guardian statues of certain Eastern temples and of the gargoyles which protect so many Western churches. At a signal from the High Priest the temple doors open: it is the actors who form the walls stamping and moving outward so as to reveal the inner pentagon. When the gates have reached their maximum opening, the priests swoosh from behind the Mammon statue, slashing in the air as if with knives. They approach the victim. The High Priest circles the heart of the victim with his fingers, gesturing in the form of a knife. All of the priests raise their knife-like hands high and plunge toward the victim, but in midair are deflected magically by the victim's rising toward them offering his throat. There is no explanation. The priests fall backward, overcome; their hands change from the gesture indicating a knife to a gesture indicating a blessing. The priests bless the victim. The walls of the pentagon crumble, the stone gargoyles magically brought to tender life. (Blackout.)

It is The Vision of the Magic Love Zap. It is The Vision of the Non-Violent Conquest of the Pentagon.

Action VI

This Text is spoken in the blackout.

Capetown. Birmingham.

How The Rite of Opposite Forces and The Vision of the Magic Love Zap lead to The Revolution of Transformation.

Free theatre. In which imagination can take power.

Capetown. Birmingham. The heart of darkness.

The heart administrates the circulation of the blood.

Be the heart. Act. Find the pain. Feel it. Make the sound of it.

The heart of Africa.

The sacred heart.

Be the revolutionist after the sexual revolution. What color is he?

Be tender hearted.

Free theatre. It is the theatre of chance.

Be the gold. Be the miners.

Play the great transformation of Capetown and Birmingham.

What happens when the revolutionaries confront the great opposing camp?

Be the great opposing camp.

Be the Bantus rising and spreading. Be the Uncle Toms. Be the black cops.

Be the music of Africa.

Enact the impulses of the collective unconscious.

Note: In place of the designation "Birmingham" the name of the black ghetto, if there is one, in the city in which the play is being performed is used.

Lights go up on stage and in the house.

The Action leads to The Revolution of Transformation. The reference here is to that period in the revolutionary struggle which is called The Struggle Period. Coming after The Revolution of Action, it raises the problems which the revolutionaries must face when the reactionary forces try to destroy the accomplishments of The Revolution with force and violence. The question is: How does the non-violent revolutionary overcome?

The Action takes as long as the energy sustains it and at its conclusion the lights dim down to darkness. (Blackout.)

THE REVOLUTION OF
TRANSFORMATION

After The Revolution of Action, The Struggle Period begins. Now the reactionary forces confront The Revolution with violence. The non-violent revolutionary will confront this destructive force with the strength of his love force and with the knowledge and wisdom which have become his through previous revolutionary experience. With the personal example of the achievements of the revolutions which have already transpired and with his newly developing human character he confronts the great opposing camp. The work of The Revolution now is the transformation of the people of the great opposing camp, and the transformation of the relationship between the revolutionaries of the new society and the militants of the customs of the past.

GUIDES

The I Ching

OF THE RITE OF OPPOSITE FORCES, THE I CHING SAYS:

THE CALDRON

———————
—— ——
———————
———————
———————
—— ——

The present hexagram refers to the cultural superstructure of society. Here it is the wood that serves as nourishment for

the flame, the spirit. All that is visible must grow beyond itself, extend into the realm of the invisible. Thereby it takes
on its true consecration and clarity and takes firm root in
the cosmic order. The fate of fire depends on wood; as long
as there is wood below, the fire burns above. It is the same
in human life; there is in man likewise a fate that lends power
to his life. And if he succeeds in assigning the right place to
life and to fate, thus bringing the two into harmony, he puts
his fate on a firm footing. These words contain hints about
the fostering of life as handed on by oral tradition in the
secret teachings of Chinese Yoga.

THE LINES:

The "ting" has yellow handles, golden carrying rings. Perseverance furthers.

The yellow handles of the "ting" are central, in order to
receive what is real.

This line is centrally placed in the upper trigram Li; it is
moreover the middle line of the trigram K'un, which is associated with the color yellow. The carrying rings are of metal:
the handle is hollow and can therefore receive the "real"
carrying rings, and the vessel can be carried.

In the language of symbols this means a great deal. The ruler
is "hollow" (receptive), hence capable of receiving the
power, that is, the teachings of the sage. Thereby he makes
progress.

THE IMAGE:

Fire over wood:
The image of The Caldron.
Thus the superior man consolidates his fate
By making his position correct.

Fire over wood is the image not of the "ting" itself but of its
use. Fire burns continuously when wood is under it. Life
must also be kept alight. In order to remain so conditioned
that the sources of life are perpetually renewed. Obviously
the same is true of the life of a community or of a state.

OF THE VISION OF THE MAGIC LOVE ZAP,
THE I CHING SAYS:

BEFORE COMPLETION

```
————————————
————   ————
————————————
————   ————
————————————
————   ————
```

This hexagram indicates a time when the transition from disorder to order is not yet completed. The change is indeed
prepared for. This hexagram presents a parallel to spring,
which leads out of winter's stagnation into the fruitful time
of summer. With this hopeful outlook the Book of Changes
comes to its close.

THE JUDGMENT:

Before Completion. Success.

The conditions are difficult. The task is great and full of responsibility. It is nothing less than that of leading the world
out of confusion back into order. But it is a task that prom-
ises success, because there is a goal that can unite the
forces now tending in different directions.

THE LINES:

Before completion, attack brings misfortune.
It furthers one to cross the great water.

The time of transition has arrived. What is to be done? A new
situation must be created; one must engage the energies of
able helpers and in this fellowship take the decisive step—
cross the great water. Then completion will become possible.

Perseverance brings good fortune.
Remorse disappears.
Shock, thus to discipline the Devil's Country.

Now it is the time of struggle. The transition must be completed. We must make ourselves strong in resolution; this
brings good fortune. All misgivings that might arise in such

grave times of struggle must be silenced. It is a question of a fierce battle to break and to discipline the Devil's Country, the forces of decadence.

The light of the superior man is true.
Good fortune.

The victory has been won. The power of steadfastness has not been routed. Everything has gone well. The new time has arrived. The new era appears all the more glorious by contrast with the misery of the old.

This hexagram comes at the end of the Book of Changes. It points to the fact that every end contains a new beginning. Thus it gives hope to men. The Book of Changes is a book of the future.

OF THE ACTION LEADING TO THE REVOLUTION OF TRANSFORMATION, THE I CHING SAYS:

PEACE

This hexagram denotes a time in nature when heaven seems to be on earth. Inside, at the center, in the key position is the light principle; the dark principle is outside. Thus the light has a powerful influence, while the dark is submissive. Here the small, weak, and evil elements are about to take their departure, while the great, strong, and good elements are moving up.

THE LINES:

Bearing with the uncultured in gentleness,
Fording the river with resolution,
Not neglecting what is distant.

It is important above all to possess enough greatness of soul to bear with imperfect people. Factionalism and the dominance of cliques are especially to be avoided.

No plain not followed by a slope.
No going not followed by a return.
He who remains persevering in danger
Is without blame.

Evil can indeed be held in check but not permanently abolished. It always returns. This conviction might induce melancholy, but it should not; it ought only to keep us from falling into illusion when good fortune comes. If we continue mindful of the danger, we remain persevering and make no mistakes. As long as a man's inner nature remains stronger and richer than anything offered by external fortune, as long as he remains inwardly superior to fate, fortune will not desert him.

Use no army now.

The wall of the town sinks back into the moat from which it was dug. We should . . . not try to stave it off by violent resistance. Should we persevere in trying to resist the evil in the usual way, our collapse would only be more complete.

The Hasidic Rungs

OF THE RUNG OF LOVE, THE HASIDIM SAY:

"When senseless hatred reigns on earth, and men hide their faces from one another, then heaven is forced to hide its face. But when love comes to rule the earth, and men reveal their faces to one another, then the splendor of God will be revealed."

"Question: We are commanded to love our neighbor as ourselves. How can I do this if my neighbor has wronged me?

"Answer: You must understand these words rightly. Love your neighbor as something which you yourself are. For all souls are one. Each is a spark from the original soul, and this soul is inherent in all souls, just as your soul is inherent in all the members of your body. It may come to pass that your hand will make a mistake and strike you. But would you then take a stick and chastise your hand because it lacked understanding and so increase your pain? It is the same if your neighbor who is of one soul with you wrongs you because of his lack of understanding. If you punish him, you only hurt yourself.

"Question: But if I see a man who is wicked before God, how can I love him?

"Answer: Don't you know that the primordial soul came out of the essence of God, and that every human soul is a part of God? And will you have no mercy on man, when you see that one of his holy sparks has been lost in a maze and is almost stifled?"

"Rabbi Mikhal gave this command to his sons: 'Pray for your enemies that all may be well with them. And should you think that this is not serving God, rest assured that, more than all our prayers, this love is indeed the service of God.' "

"We should also pray for the wicked among the peoples of the world; we should love them too. As long as we do not pray in this way, as long as we do not love in this way, the Messiah will not come."

"To love God truly, one must first love man. And if anyone tells you that he loves God and does not love his fellow-man, you will know that he is lying."

"He who thrusts his neighbor away is thrusting himself away. And even more: he who thrusts away even the smallest jot of the whole, is thrusting all of the whole away from himself."

The Colors

Yellow is the glow of the magic love zap
is the gold in the heart of the pentagon
is the transmutation of the gold of coin into the gold of sunlight
is the color of fear which is conquered by energetic action
is the saffron
is the color of the handles of the caldron
is the grain of corn and its mystical power
is the badge of shame linking Berlin and Capetown
is the Star of Egypt and the Jews
is the magic morning

The Chakras

THE ANAHATA CHAKRA

"In the heart is the charming Lotus, Anahata. It is like the celestial wishing-tree, bestowing even more than the suppli-cant's desire. Meditate within it on the sweet and excellent and upon the Abode of Mercy, the Stainless Lord whose two hands make the gestures which grant boons and dispel the fears of the three worlds. Here dwells Kakini, the Benefac-tress of All, her heart is softened. He who meditates on this Heart Lotus is able to protect and destroy the world. Fore-most among Yogis, he is dearer than the dearest. He is pre-eminently wise and full of noble deeds. His mind in its in-tense concentration is engrossed in thoughts of the Brahman (The Creative). He is able at will to enter another's body. [The Sat-Chakra-Nirupana]

" 'Another's body' refers to the fact that he is able at will to enter the enemy's fort or citadel even though guarded and rendered difficult of access. And he gains power by which he may render himself invisible, fly across the sky, and other similar powers. Such a one will not have enemies. . . ." [Arthur Avalon, "The Serpent Power"]

The Hamsopanishad assigns these Qualities to this Chakra: Possessiveness, Arrogance, Languor, Self-conceit, Discrimina-tion, Covetousness, Duplicity, Indecision, Regret, Hope, Anx-iety, and Endeavor.

In the Anahata Chakra resides stimulation in the sense of touch.

THE MANIPURA CHAKRA is assigned these Qualities: Shame, Treachery, Jealousy, Desire, Inertia, Melancholy, Worldliness, Ignorance, Disgust, Fear.

Commentary:
The Rite of Opposite Forces uses as its medium the sense of touch above all others. It can be said that during it the Sub-ject dissolves the sense of touch through acceptance, ac-knowledgment, and welcome. It is a form of union, as if the

physical assaults upon his body and psyche become one with him. He himself is both the toucher and the touched. Touch does not disturb. It is transcended.

It can be presumed that The Magic Love Zap or The Non-Violent Conquest of the Pentagon (fort or citadel) could be accomplished by the Stainless Lord, or the Benefactress of All, or by the person who has through the exercise of Kundalini-Yoga become one with the beings described: "whose gestures dispel the fears of the three words, who is able to protect the world, who is able to enter another's body, who will not have enemies. . . ."

Rung VI is the Rung of the heart: "The sacred heart." "Her heart is softened." "Be tender hearted."

The Revolution of Transformation and the confrontation be-tween the revolutionary and the great opposing camp (which is the essence of the problem in Action VI/Capetown) are prescribed for in the description of the Anahata Lotus.

The application of the meaning of the dissolution of the bad Qualities assigned to these Chakras is clear.

Confrontation

Fear × Energetic Action

The resistance to The Revolution of Transformation is fear. The actor seeks to transform the fear, both in himself and in the people, with all that he knows and feels manifested through energetic action.

Fear:	Energetic Action:
is the heritage	is pursuasive
is real	dispels demons
weakens	is muscular
reacts violently	persists
traps the mind	springs the locks
attacks	turns up with weird devices
cannot dance	can
closes the escape hatch	raises the roof

The Kabbalah

TIFERETH: ESSENCE AS THE BEAUTY OF ISRAEL &
AS THE HEART

OF THE SEFIRAH TIFERETH (ESSENCE) AS THE HEART,
THE ZOHAR TEACHES:

"He began by quoting the verse: 'He giveth food to all flesh, for his mercy endureth forever.' Now there are three great channels above by which the Holy One, blessed be He, manifests Himself, which are His precious mystery: the brain (Chokmah), the heart (Tifereth), and the liver (Malkuth). These organs act above in the opposite manner from those below. It is the head which first receives nourishment, which it sends on to the heart; then, when the heart is strengthened, it passes the nourishment on to the brain; while to the other parts of the body the liver apportions the amounts necessary. On a fast day, man sacrifices his food, his blood, heart and soul, to the supernal 'Liver'; that 'Liver' in turn offers it to the 'Heart'; in turn the 'Heart' offers it to the 'Brain,' which rules over the whole body; then the 'Liver' apportions to all the lower parts its share. At another time it is the Brain which receives first and gives to the Heart, which again, gives to the Liver and the Liver to all the lower members; and when it gives nourishment to this world it gives first to the heart, which on earth must naturally be fed first. . . . Then they sat down to eat." [The Zohar, Book IV, 153a]

Commentary:
This clarifies for the actor the dual role of the Sefirah Tifereth on Rungs V and VI. When the rabbis speak here of the "Essence" as the Heart they speak still in terms of human nourishment. The relation between The Revolution of Action ("Feed all the people") and The Revolution of Transformation ("The heart administrates the circulation of the blood") is established.

This passage also provides an insight into the physical exchanges of The Rite of Opposite Forces.

RUNG VII
The Rung of Heaven and Earth

How
The Rite of New Possibilities
and
The Vision of the Landing on Mars
lead to
Action VII: Hanoi/Saigon: (A group of people are living
in an anarchist society. What
are they doing?)

and
THE REVOLUTION OF BEING:
Glimpses of the Post-Revolutionary World

Physical Focus: The Throat

I Ching Oracles: For the Rite: Standstill
For the Vision: Decrease
For the Action: Conflict

Color: Spectrum

Chakra: Visuddha

Confrontation: Illusion × Creative Energy

Kabbalistic Sefirah: Binah (Understanding)

Rite VII
THE RITE OF NEW POSSIBILITIES

LIGHT: the darkness of outer space

In the darkness the actors reach as far as they can toward the creation of new sounds and new sound relationships. They listen closely to one another; they experiment in the use of their vocal chords and voice boxes in creating sounds and sound relationships which are, so far as they are consciously aware, not in their usual range of sounds. Sounds made by the public are included by the actors into the fabric of the whole. The sound of this Rite leads to the landing on Mars.

Vision VII
THE VISION OF THE LANDING ON MARS

LIGHT: the darkness of outer space

In the darkness five actors come from the back of the theatre in a formation arranged to resemble a Spaceship. They carry small lights or lanterns. They move slowly. Actors representing the Moon, Mars, Saturn, and Pluto carrying small lights with which they illuminate their faces move slowly through the theatre. Another actor, his body strung with small lights, plays a distant galaxy. When he moves, his limbs form constellations rotating in space. The Spaceship moves past all these celestial bodies toward the distant Planet in another galaxy. It is also Mars. It is composed of a cluster of actors carrying small lights or lanterns of many colors moving slowly from the rear of the stage. The Spaceship and the Planet approach each other. As the Spaceship moves through the theatre, the actors who form the ship speak.

to unfold the secret causes

beyond my power

blazes

unseen energy

calm air

the atoms rush

the flesh of any living thing

moon

that smokey torch of

so it is with men

the poverty of our native tongue to describe

we are all sprung from heavenly seed

mars

nevertheless the earth remains fixed in the middle of our world

whirl

fiery bodies

centaurs

herbs and cereals

saturn

life and mind

to have been created

give your mind now to the truth

movements and shapes of atoms

pluto

then many signs of death began to appear

the eighth kindling

it is autumn in the starlit dome

the liquid amplitude of the ocean prairies

two fronted night

another galaxy

the awning stretches over a large theatre

what we have never seen

the all-embracing firmament

by a frontal assault

concentrated bowls of energy

curving lips

various breeds of moon and lustrous creatures*

As the last two words are spoken the actors playing the Spaceship merge with the actors playing the distant Planet. The actors make a high sound and disperse rapidly in all directions.

IMAGE: Voyage into outer space, inner space, in which the unimaginable is encountered and understood.

Action VII

LIGHT: VIOLET

Hanoi/Saigon

Glimpses of the post-revolutionary world.

* The words of the Text were chosen by random selection from "The Nature of the Universe" by Lucretius, in the English translation by R. E. Latham.

How The Rite of New Possibilities and The Vision of the Landing on Mars lead to The Revolution of Being.

Hanoi/Saigon. After The Revolution. No State. No money. No barter. No law. No armies. No police. No bureaucracy. Breathe. Get high. Fly.

Free theatre. Because in the society we envisage anything that anyone does is perfect.

The breath of life.

In heaven they teach you to breathe.

Free theatre. Free being. Free life. Do anything. Do nothing. Be.

Breathe.

Expand consciousness.

Be the unalienated people.

Go far out.

LIGHT: grows: from VIOLET to SPECTRUM

The object of The Revolution of Being is the expansion of human potential. This could lead to flying.

The actors seek a high place in the theatre's architecture from which to take off. As the actor (or member of the public) prepares to fly, he breathes deeply, filling his body with air, while a rhythmic chant fills the theatre:

BREATHE...BREATHE...BREATHE...FLY

Arching his back, he thrusts his hands before him, and springs upward into the air. His flight comes to an end as he lands in the arms of the actors waiting below. (Flashout.)

The meaning of the scene is in the trusting relationship be-tween the flyer and the catcher. The catchers are in a for-mation of readiness, seven of them facing each other in a line, arms interlaced. They concentrate their gaze carefully

on the flyer and when they chant BREATHE...BREATHE...
BREATHE...FLY to him they are giving him their assurance
that he can entrust his safety in their hands. In midair, the
flyer, as he flashes out, is supported only by the impetus of
his own body and remains aware of the security of the sup-
portive community below. The public is encouraged to fly.
The scene leads toward a state of physical glow.

THE REVOLUTION OF BEING

The economic, political, and social changes effected by The Revolution of Action in addition to all of the interior changes effected in our character during all the preceding revolutionary stages must influence the development of human potential. When our relationship to the world and to each other, to our environment and to ourselves, to work and to time, to science and to nature, have been freed from the constraint and injury brought down on us by the errors of past civilization, we will be free to expand and to alter the nature of our being.

GUIDES

The I Ching

OF THE RITE OF NEW POSSIBILITIES,
THE I CHING SAYS:

STANDSTILL

———————
———————
———————
—— ——
—— ——
—— ——

THE LINES:

The standstill comes to an end.
First standstill, then good fortune.

The standstill does not last forever. However, it does not cease of its own accord. Continuous effort is necessary to maintain peace; left to itself it would change into stagnation and disintegration. This shows the creative attitude that man must take if the world is to be put in order.

OF THE VISION OF THE LANDING ON MARS,
THE I CHING SAYS:

DECREASE

———————————
————   ————
————   ————
————   ————
———————————
———————————

The direction of the way is upward. What is below is decreased, what is above is increased. When decrease has reached its goal, flowering is sure to begin. Decrease shows the cultivation of character. It shows first what is difficult and then what is easy. (The Interior Voyage)

THE LINES:

When three people journey together,
Their number decreases by one.
When one man journeys alone,
He finds a companion.

Confucius says of this line: Heaven and earth together and all things take shape and find form. Male and female mix their seed, and all creatures take shape and are born. In the Book of Changes it is said: "When three people journey together, their number decreases by one. When one man journeys alone he finds a companion." This refers to the effect of becoming one.

OF THE ACTION LEADING TO THE REVOLUTION OF BEING,
THE I CHING SAYS:

CONFLICT

```
————————————
————————————
————————————
————   ————
————————————
————    ————
```

THE LINES:

One cannot engage in conflict.

The Hasidic Rungs

OF THE RUNG OF HEAVEN AND EARTH, THE HASIDIM SAY:

"Man is always passing through two doors: out of this world and into the next, and out and in again."

"When people are merry and dance, it sometimes happens that they catch hold of someone who is sitting outside and grieving, pull him into the round and make him rejoice with them. The same happens in the heart of one who rejoices: grief and sorrow draw away from him, but it is a special virtue to pursue them with courage and to draw grief into gladness, so that all the strength of sorrow may be transformed into joy."

The Colors

Spectrum is the redemptive promise of the rainbow
         is the variation
         is the infinite possibility
         is the color of outer space
         is light through a prism
         is the ten thousand things
         is all the planets
         is the hiding place of the violet principle
         is the dazzle of the post-revolutionary glimpse
         is the wasteful diamond becoming the cutter's tool

The Chakras

THE VISUDDHA CHAKRA

"In the throat is the Lotus called Visuddha, which is pure and of a smokey purple hue. This region is the gateway of great Liberation for him who desires the wealth of Yoga and whose senses are pure and controlled. He who has attained complete knowledge of the Spirit becomes by constantly concentrating his mind on this Lotus a great Sage, eloquent and wise, and enjoys uninterrupted peace of mind. He sees past, present, and future and becomes the benefactor of all, free from disease and sorrow and long lived, the destroyer of endless dangers. . . . The Yogi, his breath controlled, is able to move all three worlds." [The Sat-Chakra-Nirupana]

This Chakra is the abode of the Goddess of Speech and of the sense of sound. Its organ of action is the mouth. The Chakra is located in the spinal region of the throat and larynx. The element associated with this Chakra is ether.

Commentary:
The Rite of New Possibilities is centered in sound, and in its creation through the use of the vocal chords and attentive listening. Ether is the traditional "carrier" of sound.

The Vision of the Landing on Mars is the vision of him who can see the future.

This is the Rung of The Revolution of Being; Anarchism's principles guide behavior in Hanoi/Saigon. It is "The Gateway of Great Liberation" and the changes indicated by The Revolution of Being are sufficiently cataloged in the description of this Lotus given in the Sat-Chakra-Nirupana.

". . . his breath controlled . . .": "The Breath of Life," "In heaven they teach you to breathe," "Breathe, breathe, breathe . . ."

Confrontation

Illusion × Creative Energy

The resistance to The Revolution of Being is illusion. The illusion, for instance, that there is nothing else to be done. The actor seeks through the medium of creative energy to unpower it.

Illusion:	Creative Energy:
is nothing	constructs
is premature satisfaction	is restless
is thinghood	sanctifies the world
is contentment	is ecstatic

The Kabbalah

BINAH means UNDERSTANDING.

BINAH is THE THROAT in the structure of Adam Kadmon.

OF THE SEFIRAH BINAH, THE ZOHAR TEACHES:

"There is according to our teaching a world above (Binah) and a world below (Malkuth)." [The Zohar, Book III, 53b]

"Rabbi Jose asked, 'How could Solomon, the wisest of men, say that all human actions are vanity? Can this be said of acts of righteousness or loving-kindness, of which it is written, "And the work of righteousness shall be peace [Isaiah, xxxii: 17]"?' However, as has been pointed out, 'all is vanity' refers to 'works that are done under the sun,' whilst the work of righteousness is 'above the sun.' So far so good. But what, then, is the meaning of 'all is breath and breaking of spirit' in regard to the 'works that are done under the sun?' Have we not been taught that breath is the basis of the world above (Binah) and the world below (Malkuth)?

"It has been explained in the following way. Every action done here below, if it is done with the intention of serving the Holy King, produces a 'breath' in the world above, and there is no breath which has no voice; and this voice becomes an intercessor before the Holy One, blessed be He. Contrariwise, every action which is not done with this purpose becomes a breath which floats about in the world, this 'breath' rolls about like a stone in a sling, and it 'breaks the spirit.' The act done and the word spoken in the service of the Holy One, however, ascend high above the sun and become a holy breath, which is the seed sowed by man in that world, and is called Zedakah (righteousness, loving-kindness). That which is called 'the glory of the Lord' gathers up the souls of that holy breath. Blessed are the righteous whose works are 'above the sun' and who sow a seed of righteousness which makes them worthy to enter the world to come." [The Zohar, Book III, 59a]

Commentary:
"In heaven they teach you to breathe."
Here we have a glimpse of the post-revolutionary world: that is, the world in which the conflict is resolved in terms of the sanctification of the breath (which is the life force). If the breath is holy the actions can only be actions of "loving-kindness."

The gentle contradiction of the rabbis in quoting Solomon's pessimistic decree "all is vanity," in refusing, as it were, the despair and the hopelessness of the wise men, sets an example for the actor/spectators/revolutionaries to insist on joyous alternatives:

This is the meaning of The Rite of New Possibilities and of The Vision of the Landing on Mars (i.e., doing the "impossible").

And how do they achieve this in the story above? By reinterpreting the points of "hangup" and rising "high above the sun" and declaring that such actions as they are advocating are not in the same category ("expand consciousness") as the old standards, for which these grim principles were set down.

("Because in the society we envisage anything that anyone does is perfect" and rises "high above the sun.")

BINAH is called THE FUTURE WORLD. [The Zohar, Book III, 98a and in many other citations]

RUNG VIII
The Rung of God and Man

How
The Rite of I and Thou
and
The Vision of Undoing the Myth of Eden
lead to
Action VIII: The Street

and
THE PERMANENT REVOLUTION:
Change!

Physical Focus: The Head

I Ching Oracles: For the Rite: Abundance (Fullness)
                 For the Vision: Pushing Upward
                 For the Action: Modesty

Color: White

Chakra: Ajna
        leading to
        Sahasrara (The Limitless Chakra)

Confrontation: Stasis Impetus

Kabbalistic Sefiroth: Chokmah (Wisdom) &
                      Kether (The Highest Achievement)
                      leading to
                      En Sof (The Endless)

Rite VIII
THE RITE OF I AND THOU

LIGHT: WHITE

From their positions at the end of The Revolution of Being, the actors begin the chant

AUM

and move to the center of the playing area. They face away from the public. The chant is deeply intoned. The actors allow themselves to be overwhelmed by the death image. It takes possession of them. They begin a rite of the enactment of death. They grow weak. Breath begins to shorten. Death has them by the throat. A film covers the eyes. Sight goes. The world is cut off. They sink (continuing to make the ritual sound) as if down into the earth. They say goodbye to the world. They seem to reach the portals of death. They give a death signal. The signal is each actor's purest statement of his here and now. It is his offering. At this moment when nothing seems to stand between him and annihilation, his signal reaches another one of the dying. Between the two moribund beings the holy spark of I and Thou ignites a life force, and signaling to each other, they strengthen this contact until the life force between them overcomes the death force in each of them, and they rise again.

IMAGE: Death forestalled in the contact between I and Thou.

Vision VIII
THE VISION OF UNDOING THE MYTH OF EDEN

LIGHT: grows brighter—BRIGHT WHITE

The actors form a tree. It is the Tree of Knowledge. The tree contains all of the information contained in the play. It re-enacts all that has been studied and experienced in the

course of the performance. The five actors who play the roles of the upper branches of the tree are carried on the shoulders of those who play the trunk of the tree.

The Text and Action should be altered at any performance to include significant text and/or action created by the actors and/or public during the preceding Rungs of the voyage.

The Rite of Guerilla Theatre:

> I'M NOT ALLOWED TO TAKE MY CLOTHES OFF.

Scream.

Rhythm and Song of the Resurrection of the American Indian:

> IF I COULD TURN YOU ON,
>
> IF I COULD DRIVE YOU OUT OF YOUR WRETCHED MIND,
>
> IF I COULD TELL YOU,
>
> I WOULD LET YOU KNOW.

The Rite of Prayer:

> HOLY ARM. HOLY FACE. HOLY SMILE.

The Vision of the Discovery of the North Pole:

Turning and spinning.

Electronic sound of the North Pole.

> THE REVOLUTION DOES NOT WANT VIOLENCE BUT LIFE.
>
> BOLIVIA:

I WANT THE REVOLUTION THAT FEEDS ALL THE STARVING BUT DOESN'T KILL ANYONE.

The Rite of Study:

Mudras.

TO BE FREE

IS TO BE FREE

TO CHANGE.

The Vision of the Creation of Life:

Sea sound.

Arms rise.

Exultant sound.

WHO WILL FORM A CELL TO TRANSFORM THE CITY OF
AVIGNON?

The Rite of Universal Intercourse:

The Vision of Apokatastasis:

Executioner and Victim.

The gun is fired.

The Victim rises.

The Rite of Prayer:

Holy Embrace.

JERUSALEM:

FUCK MEANS PEACE.

FUCK MEANS PEACE.

The Rite of Universal Intercourse:

The Rite of the Mysterious Voyage:

Flashout.

I/THOU I/THOU:

I/THOU I/THOU I/THOU I/THOU . . .

THE NON-VIOLENT ANARCHIST REVOLUTION

The Rite of Opposite Forces:

The Signal.

The Vision of the Magic Love Zap:

Stamping and swooshing of knives in the air.

Transformation: Benediction.

THE GREAT TRANSFORMATION OF CAPETOWN AND
BIRMINGHAM.

The Rite of New Possibilities:

. . . AND LUSTROUS CREATURES . . .

BREATHE...BREATHE...BREATHE...FLY.

AUM

HOW THE TREE OF KNOWLEDGE BECOMES THE TREE OF LIFE.

The tree dissolves and the actors move among the public and
stroll off the playing area toward the exits of the theatre.
They carry members of the public on their shoulders, or they
are carried by members of the public on their shoulders into
the street. . . .

Action VIII

LIGHT: In the playing area it darkens; in the auditorium it
grows light.

As the actors and public move toward the rear of the theatre,
the actors speak the Text.

The street.

Free the theatre. The theatre of the street. Free the street.

How The Rite of I and Thou and The Vision of Undoing the Myth of Eden lead to The Permanent Revolution.

The theatre is in the street. The street belongs to the people. Free the theatre. Free the street. Begin.

THE PERMANENT REVOLUTION

Change is the natural state of being. Permanent Revolution is the natural condition of Anarchism.

GUIDES

The I Ching

OF THE RITE OF I AND THOU, THE I CHING SAYS:

ABUNDANCE (FULLNESS)

```
____  ____
____  ____
_____
_____
____  ____
_____
```

THE JUDGMENT:

Be not sad.
Be like the sun at midday.

One should give light to the whole world. When the sun stands at midday, it begins to set; when the moon is full, it begins to wane. The fullness and emptiness of heaven and earth wane and wax in the course of time. How much truer this is of men, or of spirits and gods!

Abundance can endure only if ever larger groups are brought
to share in it, for only then can the movement continue without turning into its opposite.

OF THE VISION OF UNDOING THE MYTH OF EDEN,
THE I CHING SAYS:

PUSHING UPWARD

| ___ ___ |
| ___ ___ |
| ___ ___ |
| _____ |
| _____ |
| ___ ___ |

The lower trigram, Sun, represents wood, and the upper,
K'un, means the earth. Linked with this is the idea that wood
in the earth grows upward. Pushing Upward indicates a vertical ascent. The pushing upward is made possible not by
violence but by modesty and adaptability.

THE IMAGE:

Within the earth, wood grows:
The image of Pushing Upward.
Thus the superior man of devoted character
Heaps up small things (the Tree of Knowledge)
In order to achieve something high and great (the Tree of
Life).

OF THE ACTION LEADING TO THE PERMANENT
REVOLUTION, THE I CHING SAYS:

MODESTY

| ___ ___ |
| ___ ___ |
| ___ ___ |
| _____ |
| ___ ___ |
| ___ ___ |

This shows what modesty is and how it functions. K'un, the
earth, stands above. Lowliness is a quality of the earth: this

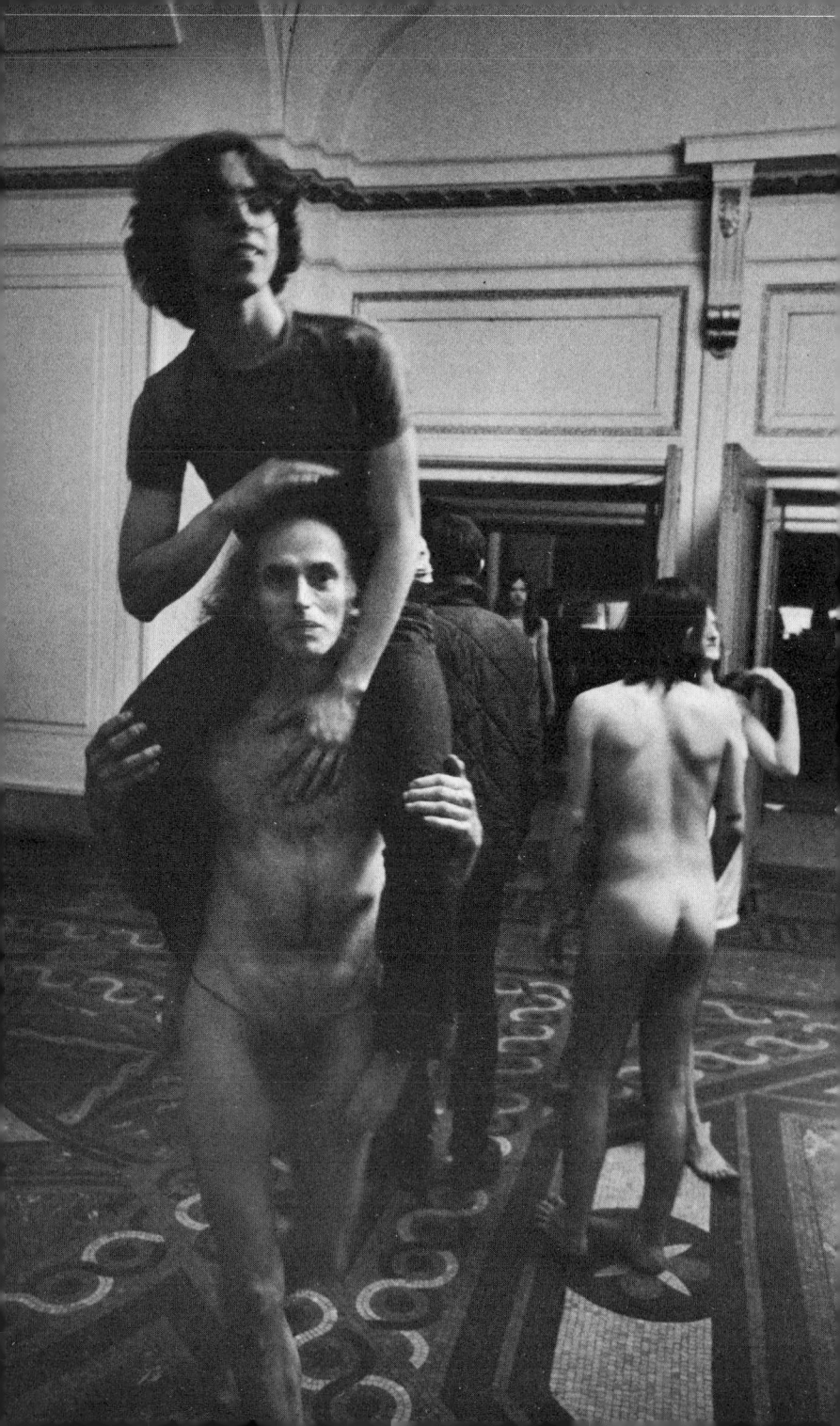

is the very reason why it appears in this hexagram as exalted, by being placed above the mountain. This shows how modesty functions in lowly, simple people (the Man in the Street): they are lifted up by it.

The Hasidic Rungs

OF THE RUNG OF GOD AND MAN, THE HASIDIM SAY:

"The understanding of man is not great enough to grasp the fact that God is beyond time. But you must understand that time exists only because we do not grasp it, only because our understanding is small. For the greater our understanding the more time is on the wane. In a dream we live seventy years and discover, on awakening, that it was a quarter of an hour. In our life, which passes like a dream, we live seventy years and then we waken to a greater understanding which shows us that it was a quarter of an hour. With our small understanding we can never grasp what we will know with the greater. Perfect understanding is beyond time."

"All joys hail from the Garden of Eden, and jests, too, provided they are uttered in true joy."

"It is written: 'The tree of life also in the midst of the garden.' Whenever a man studies or prays, he should think that he is in the garden of paradise, where there is no envy and no lust and no pride, and he will surely be safe from distraction. But how can he think in this way, since he knows that he is in this world and among people he is acquainted with? This is how: when a man studies or prays with reverence or devoutness begotten of love, and fastens and binds his spirit to God and remembers that nothing is void of him and without him, but that everything is filled with life granted by the Creator, then, in all he sees, he sees the living power of the Creator and hears his living voice. This is the meaning of the words: 'The tree of life in the midst of the garden.' He who clings to the life of God is in the midst of the garden."

"The world is a spinning die, and everything turns and changes: man is turned into angel, and angel into man, and the head into the foot, and the foot into the head. Thus all things turn and spin and change, this into that, and that into this, the topmost into the undermost, and the undermost to the topmost. For at the root all is one, and salvation inheres in the change and return of things."

The Colors

White is the purity
    is the intense flame between I and Thou
    is clarity
    is the gray-matter of the brain
    is water-clear, fluid, flexible, mercurial, changing
    is light
    is the lightning flash of insight
    is the expanding universe
    is the color of no human skin
    is the last barrier

The Chakras

THE AJNA CHAKRA

leading to

THE SAHASRARA CHAKRA (THE LIMITLESS)

"He whose spirit is nothing but a meditation on this the Ajna Lotus is able quickly to enter another's body, or another's house, at will, and becomes all-knowing and all-seeing. He realizes his unity with the Creative and acquires excellent and unknown powers. Long-lived, he ever becomes the Creator, Destroyer, and Preserver of the three worlds." [The Sat-Chakra-Nirupana]

"Progress is next made to the last or Ajna Chakra, in which are the subtle Principles of Mind and the Unmanifest Universe. The Chakra is so called because it is here that the Command (Ajna) of the Guru is received from above. It contains the great Mantra 'OM.' It 'opens the doors' to passage (through the three 'Knots' which block progress). It is a lotus of two white petals between the eyebrows. The two lobes are the cerebellum." [Arthur Avalon, "The Serpent Power"]

". . . whence all worlds derive. It is for their creation that Kundalini uncoils . . . the stages of creation (culminate in) the unitary experience in which the 'I' and 'This' coalesce in unity. . . . Experience recognizes an 'I' and 'This,' but the latter is regarded not as outside the 'I' but as part of a one self with two sides." [Avalon, ibid.]

Commentary:
The Rite of I and Thou begins with the Mantra "OM" and leads to revivification through the union of two persons, an 'I' and a 'This.'

The brain here is the source of power and inspiration, but the command for action is "the command of the Guru from above." This Guru is the Man in the Street.

THE SAHASRARA CHAKRA

The Permanent Revolution. Above the Ajna Chakra is the Sahasrara Chakra, "the Lotus with infinite petals." Of this Lotus, the Sat-Chakra-Nirupana says: "It charms. It is the chief root of Liberation. Speech, whether in prose or verse, is ever pure and sweet. Within shines the Supreme and Primordial Power graciously carrying the knowledge of the Truth to the mind of the sages, a constantly flowing stream of gladness. The Lotus is replete with every form of bliss."

In this, the highest point in Laya-Yoga ascension, the emphasis is on the expression of various degrees of joy (charm, sweetness, gladness, bliss). What does this mean to the actor? It means that in relating to the Man in the Street the temperament of joy may be the form of communication that brings great success.

Confrontation

Stasis × Impetus

The resistance to The Permanent Revolution is stasis. Here the actor's problem is to discover or invent the suitable impetus.

Stasis:	Impetus:
is impermanent	is eternal
is sterile	couples
is in its castle	is in the streets
is the Tree of Knowledge	is the Tree of Life
is the established order	inaugurates change
burns out	glows

The Kabbalah

CHOKMAH & KETHER

leading to

EN SOF.

CHOKMAH means WISDOM.

KETHER means THE HIGHEST ACHIEVEMENT.

CHOKMAH is THE BROW in the structure of Adam Kadmon.

KETHER is THE CROWN in the structure of Adam Kadmon.

Above these is
EN SOF: THE ENDLESS

OF THE SEFIRAH CHOKMAH, THE ZOHAR TEACHES:

" 'And a river went out of Eden to water the garden' [Genesis II: 10]. 'The "River," ' said Rabbi Hiya, 'is the issue of the fountain which flows perennially and from whence the whole Garden of Eden is watered, and this issue of the holy fountain is called Chokmah.' " [The Zohar, Book III, 90a]

" 'The Tree of Life also in the midst of the Garden, and The Tree of the Knowledge of Good and Evil. And the Lord God commanded. Of all the trees of the Garden thou shalt surely eat.' This means that he was permitted to eat of them all together. This tree, however, was a tree of death, in so far that he who ate of it 'by itself' was bound to die, since he took poison. Hence it says, 'In the day that thou eatest thereof thou shalt surely die,' because thereby he would be separating the shoots." [The Zohar, Book I, 35a–35b]

Commentary:
"How The Tree of Knowledge Becomes The Tree of Life";
"The Vision of Undoing the Myth of Eden":

1. A commentary by Eric Gutkind ["Choose Life"]:

"Did the Bible mean to keep Man away from knowledge?
Certainly not. The correct name of the forbidden tree was: the
'Tree of Knowledge of Good and Evil.' Did the Bible not allow Man to know how to distinguish between good and evil?
Needless to say, this is not so. But the basic document of
humanness teaches: it is not enough merely 'to know' what
is good and what is evil. Good and evil are objects of decision
and action. There is danger in making good and evil mere
neutral objects of knowledge because in 'only' knowing them
we neutralize all things. Knowledge can become destructive
if detached from ethical decision. So the admirable results
of science are misused for destruction. So the very Bible is
used for casting darkness. The mightier the truth the more
horrible may be the misuse of that truth. Certainly there can
be no ethical action without knowledge. 'The ignorant cannot
be the upright' is an old Hebrew saying. But it is just as true
that knowledge is inseparably tied to ethics. The two trees,
the Tree of Life and the Tree of Knowledge in the Garden of
Eden, were an indivisible unity of indestructible life. A profound kabbalistic teaching asserts: Man made a split between the two trees, and by that act he ruined the Garden
of Paradise. This primal schizophrenia tells in eternal terms
the story of our path of suffering through history. The primal
split is actualized in history because history is the stage
where the restoration of Man will take place. To the
'kizuz' belongs the 'tikkun': healing the split, restoring primal unity."

2. A commentary by Eric Gutkind ["The Absolute Collective"]:

"When, turning away from 'The Tree of Life' he plucked the
deadly fruit of 'The Tree of Knowledge,' which is the tree of
possessiveness—then death broke its bonds and was set
free by God. . . . For the world at its origin was no less than
Paradise (Gan Eden). . . . And when this perversion took
place, the unity of paradisaical growth was broken. . . .

The human hand, so holy in its origin, once it was stretched out to grasp and seize, became accursed. What it took (now that man had turned away from 'The Tree of Life') it stole. In all appropriation and technical craft there lurks a demon who should have been the slave but was now to be the master of man who had so idolatrously forfeited his lordship. Little by little the radiance was dimmed in which man had beheld the true world. . . . Nothing of what surrounds us, not even our own existence, is the original reality. We have about us a distorted, a perverted form of existence. What we perceive is not the real thing, though to the seeing eye Gan Eden, the lost, still glimmers through the veil of the unessential world, waiting to be delivered from its spell."

OF THE SEFIRAH KETHER, MAURICE SIMON (APPENDIX TO THE ZOHAR, SONCINO EDITION, 1931) EXPLAINS:

"The First Grade (Kether)—the 'Most Mysterious and Recondite'—indistinguishable from the EN SOF (limitless, uncharacterizable) and corresponding to absolute nothingness in the work of creation—is not directly mentioned in the scripture, unless it is alluded to by the letter Beth (meaning 'in') of the word Bereshith (meaning 'in the beginning . . .') implying that it went, so to speak, into itself, and so made a start. This start consists of a flash (Zohar), which thus releases the creative powers of the limitless. From this 'inwardness' results a point or focus capable of infinite development and expansion. . . ."

Commentary:
The Vision of Undoing the Myth of Eden takes the voyager back into the echoes of each Rung that he has passed, and then he approaches that mysterious point at which the limitations have been reached—at that moment the play and the players must move out . . . into the street.

EN SOF

This limitless, incomprehensible effulgence of Holiness radiates above the grades. Of it the Zohar only says that it is unknowable:

"En Sof cannot be known, nor how it makes beginning nor end, just as the number zero, produces beginning and end.

What is the beginning? It is the supreme point and the World-to-come." [The Zohar, Book IV, 239a]

Commentary:
The En Sof is the Mystery of the Street.

The pre-revolutionary vocabulary cannot describe the world to come. In "The Absolute Collective" Eric Gutkind described the mystery of the street as the "City Absolute":

"The absolute collective cannot be 'made,' it can only be called and summoned. Since it has always existed it needs only to be named and addressed aright in order to appear. We shall not come to it with the help of theory or technical knowledge, or with that of ideas and ideals. We can pay for it only with the coin of our own heart. We must be great hearted. The heart is not feeling, it is the center of our being. In its rapture, in the white heat of its thoughts, in its lion's might, the heart will lead us to the City Absolute in which all things are the center. It is the abode of peace, of that peace that already permeates the deeper strata of our lives. In the City Absolute there are no doors and no walls. For there all things say 'thou' and all hands are joined in an unending embrace. This is the beginning . . . Man's peace is not a final cessation of his activity. He finds it when he breaks through the barriers that divide him from his original state, where alone he can live with the matchless intensity of man who has become man indeed."

ILLUSTRATIONS

1 The Rite of Guerilla Theatre, Geneva 1968; in the background: Jean-Jacques Lebel waves a Black Flag.   18

2 The Vision of the Death and Resurrection of the American Indian; Totem Poles, Madison, Wisconsin.   20-21

3 Action I: an impromptu demonstration on stage against the occupation of Czechoslovakia. Geneva.   24-25

4 The Rite of Prayer.   35

5 The Vision of the Discovery of the North Pole.   38

6 Action II, beginning.   43

7 The Rite of Study.   55

8 The Vision of the Creation of Life.   60

9 Action III.   60-61

10 The Rite of Universal Intercourse, Bennington, Vermont.   73

11 The Vision of Apokatastasis.   76

12 Action IV, Bennington College, Vermont.   79

13 The Rite of the Mysterious Voyage.   88

14 The Vision of the Integration of the Races.   92-93

15 Action V, Chateauvallon, France: first free performance. Julian Beck and Saul Gottlieb burn money.   95

16 The Rite of Opposite Forces ("the Mat Piece").   104

17 Flashout and signal after the Rite of Opposite Forces   106-107

18 The Vision of the Magic Love Zap (exorcism of the Pentagon).   108

19 Action VI: during a performance, members of the Pageant Players enact a piece on the Presidio Mutiny trial.   110

20 Action VII, the Flying (Julian Beck, rehearsal).   126

21 The Rite of I and Thou.   134

22 The Vision of the Undoing of the Myth of Eden, the Tree
    of Knowledge and Life.   136

23 To the Street.   142

Note: no photographs are available for The Rite of New Possibilities and The Vision of Landing on Mars (Rung VII) since they are performed in total darkness.

Photographs by Gianfranco Mantegna.

CHRONOLOGY OF PERFORMANCES

July 22–23, 1968: (Preview Performances): Avignon, Cloître des Carmes

July 24, 1968: (Premiere): Avignon, Cloître des Carmes

July 25–26, 1968: Avignon, Cloître des Carmes

August 1, 1968: Ollioulles: Chateauvallon (Free Performance)

August 20–24, 1968: Geneva: Pavillon des Sports

September 26–28, 1968: New Haven, Conn.: Yale University Theatre

October 14, 16, 18–19, 1968: New York, N.Y.: Brooklyn Academy of Music (Music Hall)

October 29, 1968: Stony Brook, Long Island, N.Y.: Gymnasium, New York University

November 5, 1968: Cambridge, Mass.: Kresge Auditorium (Massachusetts Institute of Technology)

November 15, 1968: Pittsburgh, Pa.: Skibo Hall, Carnegie Mellon University

November 20, 1968: Castleton, Vt.: Gymnasium, Castleton College

November 21, 1968: Bennington, Vt.: Gymnasium, Bennington College

November 26, 1968: Philadelphia, Pa.: Fleischer Auditorium (Y.M.H.A.)

December 11, 1968: Ann Arbor, Mich.: Michigan Union Ballroom

December 17, 1968: Rochester, N.Y.: Strong Auditorium, University of Rochester

December 18, 1968: Ithaca, N.Y.: Bailey Hall, Cornell University

December 22, 1968: Boston (Roxbury), Mass.: Crown Manor

December 29, 1968/January 1, 1969: New York, N.Y.: Poe Forum (Bronx), formerly Loew's 167th Street

January 4, 1969: New York, N.Y.: Hunter College Concert Hall

January 12, 1969: Chicago, Ill.: Nadell Hall, University of Chicago

January 16, 1969: Madison, Wisc.: Meeting House, First Unitarian Church

January 24, 1969: Chicago, Ill.: The Auditorium Theatre

January 31, 1969: Kansas City, Kan.: Soldiers & Sailors Memorial Hall

February 6, 1969: Boulder, Colo.: University of Colorado Ballroom

February 14, 1969: Portland, Oreg.: Sports Center, Reed College

February 20, 1969: Berkeley, Calif.: Berkeley Community Theatre
February 28, 1969: Los Angeles, Calif.: University of Southern California, Bovard Auditorium
March 7–8, 1969: San Francisco, Calif.: Nourse Auditorium
March 22–24 & 26, 1969: New York, N.Y.: Brooklyn Academy of Music (Music Hall)
May 1, 1969: Mulhouse, France: Salle Rallye Drouot
May 6, 1969: St. Hilaire du Touvet, France: Théâtre du Sanatorium
May 10, 1969: St. Martin d'Hyères, France: Terrasse de la Bibliotèque de Droits et des Lettres, Université de Grenoble
May 31, 1969: St. Etienne, France: Comédie de St. Etienne, Salle Jean Dasté
June 9–10, 20–21, 27–28, 1969: London, England: The Roundhouse
October 20, 1969: Turin, Italy: Teatro Alfieri
October 21, 1969: Turin, Italy: Unione Culturale, Palazzo Carignano
October 31, 1969: Milan, Italy: Circo Medini
November 2, 1969: Milan, Italy: Università Politecnica
November 14–16, 1969: Prato, Italy: Teatro Metastasio
November 18, 1969: Florence, Italy: Circolo Space Electronic
November 21, 1969: Urbino, Italy: Teatro Sanzio
November 29–30, 1969: Naples, Italy: Teatro Mediteranneo
December 1, 1969: Rome, Italy: Aula III, Facoltà di Legge, Università di Roma
December 10–13, 1969: Brussels, Belgium: Théâtre 140
December 16, 1969: Seraing, Belgium: Centre Culturel
December 21–23, 1969: Brussels, Belgium: Théâtre 140
December 31, 1969/January 2, 1970: Berlin, Germany: Akademie der Künste
January 10, 1970: Berlin, Germany: Sportpalast